How to Deal With Your Bank Manager

How to Deal With Your Bank Manager

Geoffrey Sales

KOGAN PAGE

First published in Great Britain in 1988 by Kogan Page Limited, 120 Pentonville Road, London N1 9JN

British Library Cataloguing in Publication Data

Sales, Geoffrey
How to deal with your bank manager.
1. Corporations—Great Britain—Finance
2. Bank loans—Great Britain
I. Title
332.1'753 HG4135

ISBN 1-85091-596-2
ISBN 1-85091-597-0 Pbk

Printed and bound in Great Britain by
Biddles Ltd, Guildford

Contents

Preface

Now that you have got as far as opening this book, you are no doubt wondering whether there is going to be any benefit to you in buying it.

I will try to be as brief as possible. Answer me two questions:

1. Have you ever wondered what your bank manager really thinks about you and your business?
2. Have you ever thought it would be nice to be able to anticipate what your bank manager was going to say or the questions he was going to ask?

That is what this book sets out to do: to give you an insight into the bank manager's mind.

The benefit is fairly obvious. Knowing what your bank manager is thinking must be an advantage. To have all the answers at your fingertips cannot fail to impress.

Still not convinced? Stay with it a little longer. Read the Introduction and if you are still not happy, put it back and no hard feelings!

Introduction

This book is written for anyone who runs any sort of business and who needs or will need at some time in the future to talk to the bank manager about the business with a view to borrowing money.

A banker may from time to time visit you on your business premises and will get some sort of impression of how efficiently the business is run, but the main source of information will be the business's annual audited accounts.

The bank will always want to keep a copy of your audited accounts in their files irrespective of whether you are borrowing from them, but obviously if you are a borrower the manager will look at the accounts very critically.

But what is it exactly that the bank will look at? In Part 1 of this book I shall highlight the areas which a bank will examine and which are important to them. You will probably find that they are different from the things which are important to you or your accountant. I will show you the questions which your bank is likely to ask, and suggest some of the answers you might use.

In Part 2 I shall go through how a banker assesses a proposition to borrow money from the bank. Each borrower is different and will be treated on an individual basis. The specific terms and details of lending to builders, farmers, manufacturers, retailers, etc, will vary, but basically the banker's approach will be exactly the same in each case. It is this approach which will be examined in Part 2.

Part 3 is devoted to sources of finance other than traditional bank overdrafts and loans. However, your bank is the link to these other sources, as most banks have subsidiary companies which specialise in these areas.

Businesses have to start somewhere. Many new businesses are started every year and in Part 4 I shall point out the particular problems which you might have in getting a banker to lend money on a new venture. If you are a newcomer to business, it will be better to start by reading Part 4.

The objectives of this book are that, after reading it, all business people will be able to:

(a) Identify the information in a balance sheet which a banker will regard as important.
(b) Interpret that information in the same way as the banker interprets it.
(c) Anticipate the questions which a banker will ask arising from the information in the balance sheet, and be able to provide the answers and any other supporting information.
(d) Identify the factors which a banker will consider when assessing a proposition to lend money to a business.
(e) Identify other bank services which will be of benefit to a business.

One of the major reasons why banks refuse to lend is not because the proposition is unsound but because the customers have not presented the facts as clearly as they might have. Knowing how bankers think and how they approach their jobs will undoubtedly be a tremendous advantage to you.

Part 1
The Balance Sheet

1. Introduction

How useful is it?

A banker is just as aware as you are that a balance sheet gives very limited information about a business. It shows the position of the business at just one day in the year, but the current assets and current liabilities change every day. For example, on the day following balance sheet date, you might take delivery of £20,000 of stock which will obviously increase the stock figure and also increase either creditors or bank overdraft.

Trends

If he is to make a reasonable assessment, the banker must have at least two and preferably three years' balance sheets so that the trend of the business can be established. Looking at one balance sheet in isolation is as pointless as my asking myself if I am young or old. To my son I am ancient and boring but to my father I am quite young and irresponsible. It depends from where you are looking. A profit of £1000 will look poor if in the previous year £5000 was made, but it will look quite good if in the previous year a loss was made.

Interim figures

In times gone by, the only information a banker would require would be the annual balance sheet, but things change so quickly nowadays that bankers find this insufficient. A lot can happen to a business in a year and bankers often make it a condition of lending that you provide figures for current assets and current liabilities on a quarterly or even monthly basis.

Why are these figures required? Well, it is in the composition of current assets and liabilities that the first signs of trading losses will be seen and the banker will want an early warning of this so that a decision can be made as to how best to protect the bank's position. Without regular figures the losses would not be noticed until the audited accounts were produced at the year end, by which time it might be too late. It is, of course, in your interests too that potential losses can be identified quickly so that corrective action can be taken.

These are often referred to as management figures and we shall come back to them later, but let us first look at the balance sheet itself – what a banker looks at, and the questions which are likely to be asked.

Method to be used

Rather than talk about this in general terms, it would probably be more interesting to look at the balance sheets of three fictitious businesses as a base for bringing out the various points. These balance sheets are taken from questions in the Chartered Institute of Bankers examinations which are the examinations your bank manager has to pass. At the bottom of each you will see information supplied which would come from the profit and loss account. The banker will no doubt want to see your P & L account in addition to your balance sheet but the only purpose it serves is to show how well you are controlling the overheads of your business.

GREEN LIGHT ELECTRICAL COMPANY LTD
Balance Sheet as at 30 June

		Last Year		This Year
	£	£	£	£
Freehold land & buildings		60,000		60,000
Plant & equipment		30,000		28,000
Motor vehicles		40,000		42,000
		130,000		130,000
Stock	420,000		460,000	
Debtors	240,000		270,000	
	660,000		730,000	
Directors' Loan a/c	50,000		30,000	
Creditors	400,000		450,000	
Bank	110,000		160,000	
	560,000		640,000	
Net Current Assets		100,000		90,000
Net Assets		£230,000		£220,000
Financed by:				
Capital		50,000		50,000
Profit & loss		180,000		170,000
		£230,000		£220,000

	Last Year	This Year
Sales	2.35M	2.45M
Gross Profit	162,000	145,000
Net Profit (loss)	5,000	(10,000)
After: Depreciation	16,000	16,000
Directors' remuneration	36,000	35,000

Quarterly figures subsequent to latest year's Balance Sheet

	September	December	March
	£	£	£
Directors' Loan a/c	30,000	30,000	20,000
Debtors	265,000	240,000	235,000
Stock	460,000	465,000	460,000
Creditors	450,000	445,000	460,000
Bank	165,000	165,000	175,000

FIRE TYRES LTD
Balance Sheet as at 31 December

	Year Before		Last Year		This Year	
	£	£	£	£	£	£
Land & buildings	4,200		4,800		6,900	
Machinery & plant	18,300		15,700		24,400	
Goodwill	2,700		2,700		2,700	
Fixed Assets		25,200		23,200		34,000
Cash			200		17,300	
Debtors	34,400		61,800		20,700	
Stock	23,000		43,200		39,000	
	57,400		105,200		77,000	
Creditors	29,800		55,000		52,000	
Bank	22,700		39,700		–	
Loan from directors	9,500		7,800		7,800	
Current tax	2,100		–		8,000	
	64,100		102,500		67,800	
Net Current Assets		(6,700)		2,700		9,200
		18,500		25,900		43,200
Financed by:						
Capital		100		100		100
Profit & loss		18,400		25,800		43,100
		18,500		25,900		43,200
Sales		165,000		322,000		295,000
Gross profit		55,000		80,000		115,000
Net profit		3,600		7,400		17,300
After: Depreciation		4,500		4,400		7,400
Tax		4,700		5,300		12,700
Directors' remuneration		15,000		16,000		18,000

AB EQUIPMENT
Balance Sheet as at 31 March

	Year Before		Last Year		This Year	
		£		£		£
Fixed Assets						
Goodwill		3,000		3,000		3,000
Vehicles		8,000		7,000		9,000
Fixtures & fittings		2,500		2,250		2,000
Plant & machinery		6,000		4,500		6,500
		19,500		16,750		20,500
Current Assets						
Bank	3,000		4,500		2,000	
Debtors	22,500		24,750		25,000	
Stock	10,000		12,000		20,000	
Work-in-progress	2,000		2,500		3,000	
	37,500		43,750		50,000	
Current Liabilities						
HP creditors	5,000		4,000		7,000	
Trade/sundry creditors	10,000		12,000		14,000	
Current tax	3,000	19,500	2,000	25,750	4,000	25,000
		39,000		42,500		45,500
Capital Accounts		36,000		39,000		42,500
Profits		3,000		3,500		3,000
		39,000		42,500		45,500
Sales		90,000		99,000		108,000
Cost of sales						
Labour		30,000		34,200		39,000
Materials		15,000		17,250		19,700
		45,000		51,450		58,700
Gross Profit		45,000		47,550		49,300
Net Profit		3,000		3,500		3,000
After: Drawings		25,000		25,000		25,000
Rent		1,500		1,500		1,500
Depreciation		1,500		2,000		2,500

Note: The capital account of each partner would normally be shown, but a combined figure is shown here for purposes of clarity.

2. Net Worth

What is it?

The net worth of a business is exactly as it sounds – the value of the business after all liabilities have been paid. In other words, what it is worth to you as proprietor. The banker will include such obvious items as capital, reserves and accumulated profits in the profit and loss account but will also make some adjustments. There may be loans shown on the liabilities side of the balance sheet (eg, directors' loans) and the banker would ask if these could be regarded as part of the capital. Indeed, the bank will often make it a condition of lending to you that directors' loans are capitalised or at least that you give an undertaking that repayment of directors' loans will not be given priority over repayment of the bank borrowing. Alternatively, there might be loans from members of your family and the bank would want to know the terms on which this money has been borrowed and when it has to be repaid. Depending on the terms, the bank might be prepared to regard such loans as part of the permanent capital.

Adjustments made by the bank

If the business owns the premises from which it operates either on a freehold or long leasehold basis, then it could be that the value of these premises shown in the balance sheet is less than the true market value. If the true value were shown in the balance sheet this would increase the value of the business – ie a capital reserve would be created. The bank would not ask you to show the true value but they would certainly take the true value into account when assessing the net worth of your business. The bank would regard the difference between market value and balance sheet value as a 'hidden reserve'.

A different attitude is taken to short-term leases – say 21 years or less. These depreciate in value as the term of the lease expires and the bank would expect that fact to be shown in the balance sheet. If it is not shown then the bank will make their own downward adjustment, which will have the effect of reducing the value of the business.

Importance of net worth

Why is the net worth of a business important to the bank? Well, a bank is highly unlikely to lend more than a business is worth; indeed, it will expect to lend a good deal less than the net worth. There are exceptions, of course, the most notable of which are small 'one man band' businesses such as self-employed plumbers, property repairers etc, where the business has very few assets. In these situations the bank is not really lending to the business but lending to the man, and he would have to provide personal security.

Let us look at our three balance sheets and see what the banker would make of them.

Green Light Electrical Company Ltd

	Last Year	This Year
	£	£
Capital	50,000	50,000
P & L	180,000	170,000
	230,000	220,000
+ Directors' Loans	50,000	30,000
	280,000	250,000

(a) The P & L account has reduced by £10,000, which reflects a net loss of £10,000 on the latest year's trading. The bank will want to know why. If you can convince them that it is a 'one-off' due to exceptional circumstances then the bank will be less concerned than if it appeared that the business was in trouble of a more permanent nature. The reason for the bank's concern is obvious – if a business is making losses then the bank begin to doubt the business's ability to repay the money borrowed from them.

(b) Directors' loans have reduced by £20,000. The bank will want to know why. If the directors start to withdraw the money which is due to them, then the bank, while appreciating their right to do so, would be unable to avoid the thought that the directors might be getting their money out while they still can. In other words, there is the suspicion that all is not well. There might be a perfectly logical explanation but, allied to the fact that a loss of £10,000 was made, the bank would be a little uneasy and would question the directors in some detail. Also, in these circumstances the bank would probably not regard directors' loans as part of the net worth.

(c) The bank would therefore regard the present net worth of the business as no more than £220,000. If bank lending was no more than (say) £150,000, then the bank would not be unduly worried about that relationship provided you could convince them of your ability to stop the slide and reverse the trend.

(d) The bank would note that the freehold land and buildings is quoted at the same figure in both years. They might ask when the premises were last valued professionally and what that valuation was, because it could be that there is a hidden reserve in that asset which would of course boost the net worth.

Fire Tyres Ltd

	Year Before	Last Year	This Year
	£	£	£
Capital	100	100	100
P & L	18,400	25,800	43,100
	18,500	25,900	43,200
Directors' Loans	9,500	7,800	7,800
	28,000	33,700	51,000
Less Goodwill	2,700	2,700	2,700
	25,300	31,000	48,300

(a) The increasing balance in P & L account shows the company is making and retaining good profits in the business.

(b) Directors' loans reduced slightly last year, but in view of the increasing P & L account the bank would not be concerned and would be unlikely even to mention it.

(c) The bank will deduct goodwill from the figure for net worth because if the bank are trying to recover their money when the company has gone into liquidation, then goodwill will be worthless.

(d) The net worth might be further boosted by any hidden reserve in land and buildings.

(e) The present net worth of £48,300 (ignoring any possible hidden reserve) could encourage the bank to lend (say) £30,000 quite happily – especially as the trend is upwards.

AB Equipment

	Year Before	Last Year	This Year
	£	£	£
Capital Accounts	36,000	39,000	42,500
Profits	3,000	3,500	3,000
	39,000	42,500	45,500
Less Goodwill	3,000	3,000	3,000
	36,000	39,500	42,500

(a) Only slight increases in profits, showing a rather modest performance.

(b) Goodwill would be deducted, for reasons already mentioned.

(c) No hidden reserves.

(d) Present net worth £42,500 but against an apparent background of a rather sluggish business, any bank borrowing in excess of (say) £20,000 would be generous of the bank.

3. Current Assets

The bank will be interested in the relationship between current assets and current liabilities, and they will want to see a net surplus. This should indicate that the business is capable of meeting its day-to-day liabilities without too much trouble. Obviously, a business which has a cash shortage and is unable to satisfy a pressing debt is very vulnerable indeed.

The bank will be extremely concerned if they see a deterioration in the situation. For example, let us assume that a business has the following:

	£
Current Assets	20,000
Current Liabilities	10,000
Surplus	10,000

If the business borrows £10,000 from its bank to purchase extra stock then both current assets and current liabilities would increase by £10,000, giving the following position:

	£
Current Assets	30,000
Current Liabilities	20,000
Surplus	10,000

The surplus remains the same because both changes have been in the *current* section of the balance sheet. But suppose the business borrowed £10,000 from the bank not to buy stock but to buy machinery; there would then be an increase of £10,000 in *current* liabilities but the corresponding increase would be in *fixed* assets, not *current* assets. The following would result:

	£
Current Assets	20,000
Current Liabilities	20,000
Surplus	nil

The surplus has disappeared – a considerable deterioration in the current assets/current liabilities relationship. However, the bank would not be too worried if the reduction is due to fixed asset purchase, but if no fixed assets have been bought then the worsened situation must be due to losses on trading. Therefore, if your net current assets position is weakening, be prepared to be questioned about it.

Current asset ratio

The bank might sometimes use a ratio to assess more accurately the relationship of current assets to current liabilities, ie current assets divided by current liabilities.

In our original example where £10,000 was borrowed from the bank to purchase stock we saw that the surplus remained the same, but in fact the ratio of current assets to current liabilities weakened:

Before transaction

	£	
Current Assets	20,000	
Current Liabilities	10,000	Ratio 2:1

After transaction

	£	
Current Assets	30,000	
Current Liabilities	20,000	Ratio 1.5:1

In other words, although the surplus is unchanged, the current liabilities are now only covered 1.5 times instead of twice by current assets.

How do our three businesses shape up?

Green Light Electrical Company Ltd

		Last Year	This Year
		£	£
	Current Assets	660,000	730,000
(Less)	Current Liabilities	510,000	610,000
	Surplus	150,000	120,000

(a) Directors' loans have been excluded from current liabilities because banks usually regard them as part of the net worth.

However, in Green Light's case, the bank might well have left them in current liabilities. If they had, then the surplus would have fallen from £100,000 to £90,000 (as shown in the balance sheet).

(b) In this case, of course, the bank can actually see that a loss has been made, but if a similar position had been revealed by management figures (ie quarterly or monthly figures for current assets and current liabilities with no profit or loss figure shown) then the bank would be asking you some serious questions, namely is it fixed asset investment or loss? We have management figures for this company which we will examine shortly.

(c) The ratio has fallen from 1.29:1 to 1.19:1 (if directors' loans are excluded from current liabilities) and from 1.17:1 to 1.14:1 (if included). In Green Light's case, the ratios are far less significant than the actual figures.

Fire Tyres Ltd

	Year Before	Last Year	This Year
	£	£	£
Current Assets	57,400	105,200	77,000
(Less) Current Liabilities	54,600	94,700	60,000
Surplus	2,800	10,500	17,000

(a) Again, directors' loans have been excluded from current liabilities.

(b) The surplus is increasing each year, indicating a business which is trading profitably.

(c) Just as a deterioration in the net current asset position can be caused by big investment in fixed assets, so an improvement in net current assets can be created by under-investment in fixed assets. The banker would have a quick look to see if the current position has been 'window dressed' in this way. Certainly, in 'Last Year's' figures, fixed assets reduced from the previous year from £25,200 to £23,200, ie a reduction of £2000, but this is after depreciation of £4400. Therefore, there was an investment in fixed assets of £2400, which looks very low. The banker might comment on that and therefore you should be prepared with an answer – the most probable one is that there was no need for any further investment. The banker might let it go without comment in view of the substantial investment 'This Year' of £18,200, ie fixed assets have grown from £23,200 to £34,000, an increase of £10,800 after depreciation of £7400 = £18,200.

(d) However, this business is in a strong net current asset position.

(e) There are a couple of other things the bank would mention. First, why no tax 'Last Year', and second, how has the business managed 'This Year' to rid itself of bank borrowing and build up a cash surplus? It could well have something to do with the drastic reduction in the level of debtors, eg the company might be doing more business on a cash instead of a credit basis by offering discounts for cash settlements.

AB Equipment

	Year Before	Last Year	This Year
	£	£	£
Current Assets	37,500	43,750	50,000
(Less) Current Liabilities	18,000	18,000	25,000
	19,500	25,750	25,000

(a) A reasonable increase in the middle year but a slight reduction in the latest figures. The bank would want to know why.

(b) Once again, the increase in the middle year seems to be at the expense of fixed assets which have reduced £2750 while depreciation is only £2000, suggesting the sale of some asset. The bank would question this.

(c) The slight reduction in net current assets 'This Year' obviously reflects the investment in fixed assets of £6250, ie an increase in balance sheet figures of £3750 (£16,750 to £20,500) after deducting depreciation of £2500. The investment has been partly financed by an increase in HP.

(d) Not a lot to say about this business. The bank can just about answer their own questions but they will still want to hear it from you.

Management figures

Let us return to Green Light Electrical Company Ltd. because we can see that quarterly figures are being produced for current assets and current liabilities. The bank have obviously advanced money to this company on condition that these figures are provided.

Early warning of trouble

Why do banks want these figures? Because it is in these figures that the first signs of unprofitable trading will be seen. The actual causes of unprofitable trading could be any one or a combination of such things as falling sales, reduction in margins due to competition, rising overheads etc (these will be discussed later) but they will be *reflected* in the current assets/current liabilities relationship.

Without these figures it would be some time after the year end when the audited accounts were produced before the bank (and you too probably) were aware that a loss had been made. The regular compilation of this information gives you the chance to correct any problems before they become too big.

Example

To illustrate how profits and losses will bring about increases and decreases respectively in the net current assets position let us look at a simple example at the lowest basic level.

Assume you borrow £10 from the bank and you buy £10-worth of stock. You have a current asset of £10 and a current liability of £10. You sell the stock for £12, ie 20 per cent profit. What do you do with the £12? You could buy £12-worth of stock, which then means you have a current asset of £12 and a current liability of £10 – a surplus of £2. Or you could just replace the stock for £10 and reduce your borrowing from the bank to £8, giving you current assets of £10 and current liabilities of £8 – a surplus of £2. The profit element must always either increase current assets or reduce current liabilities unless it is used to buy fixed assets or you withdraw all the profit for yourself. If you always did the latter then your business would just stagnate.

Let us now assume that your suppliers increase their prices to £11 from £10, and because of fierce competition you cannot increase your selling price beyond £12 without losing business. Your profit element is now only £1 and for each £12-worth of sales you can either increase your current assets or reduce your current liabilities by only £1 instead of £2.

Bringing it back up to full scale now, it has to be appreciated that not all your creditors are suppliers. Some of them will be fixed costs, eg rent, rates etc. These will continue to increase and your smaller profit element might be insufficient to pay them. It is then that the surplus disappears completely and deficits appear, in other words, current liabilities exceed current assets.

Turning to Green Light's management figures the following situation emerges:

	September	December	March
	£	£	£
Current Assets			
(Debtors and Stock)	725,000	705,000	695,000
Current Liabilities			
(Creditors and Bank)	615,000	610,000	635,000
Surplus	110,000	95,000	60,000

As we can see, the surplus is falling dramatically and the bank will be extremely concerned. Unless fixed assets have been purchased, it means that substantial losses have been made over a nine-month period. If you were the directors of this business, you could expect to be questioned very seriously about your plans for stopping this slide and returning to profitable trading.

The bank would look at their security position because this situation is so grave that they might well have to demand repayment of their lending before the situation gets any worse. An urgent meeting would be called with the directors before any action was implemented to realise the security. To save the business, they would have to convince the bank of their ability to put matters right.

4. Acid Test

We have seen the bank looking at the relationship between current assets and current liabilities, and have noted that the bank like to see a good surplus of net current assets. Not all the assets grouped under the heading 'current assets' are particularly liquid in the true sense of the word. If stock is raw materials which have to go through a manufacturing process and then be sold on credit terms, it could be a few months before the amount represented by stock is converted into available cash for the business. This is not true of all businesses. The stock of a retailer, for example, will be represented by goods on shelves which can be sold immediately.

To test the true liquidity of a business, the bank will look at the relationship of the liquid assets (in the true sense of the word) and the current liabilities. This is a severe test but it should highlight the business's *real* ability to meet day-to-day liabilities from assets which are cash (or near cash, like debtors). In other words, assets such as stock and work-in-progress will be eliminated from the calculation, although, as already stated, a strong argument could be put forward for a retailer's stock to be included.

The ideal situation would be for liquid assets to cover all current liabilities, but what is more important to the bank is that there is no marked deterioration in the relationship from one year to the next.

Green Light Electrical Company Ltd

	Last Year	This Year
	£	£
Debtors	240,000	270,000
(Less) Current Liabilities	510,000	610,000
Deficit	(270,000)	(340,000)

(a) A big increase in the deficit of £70,000, which is symptomatic of the difficulties this company is experiencing. The bank would be very concerned and would want your plans for putting matters right.

(b) Directors' loans have been excluded from the calculation.

Fire Tyres Ltd

	Year Before	Last Year	This Year
	£	£	£
Cash and Debtors	34,400	62,000	38,000
(Less) Current Liabilities	54,600	94,700	60,000
Deficit	(20,200)	(32,700)	(22,000)

(a) An inconsistent picture. The bank would want to know why the middle year was so much less liquid than the other two years. Compare this with the situation when all the current assets were used – then we saw a steadily improving situation year by year. In point of fact the ratio of cash and debtors to current liabilities *is* consistent, at just over 0.6:1, and therefore the bank are unlikely to worry, especially as an improved position in cash terms is showing in the latest year's accounts.

(b) Sales almost doubled in the middle year and we saw each of the main current assets and current liabilities increasing in similar proportions (more or less). This obviously results in the increase in the deficit in the middle year. In the third year, however, sales have declined slightly but debtors have reduced considerably, and the bank borrowing has been converted into a cash surplus. As stated earlier this is probably due to discounts being offered for cash settlements. The saving in bank interest has contributed to the increase in net profit. Obviously, the business has streamlined itself in the latest year.

(c) The bank would be happy with this situation.

AB Equipment

	Year Before	Last Year	This Year
	£	£	£
Bank and Debtors	25,500	29,250	27,000
(Less) Current Liabilities	18,000	18,000	25,000
Surplus	7,500	11,250	2,000

(a) A significant reduction in the latest year. Compare the current assets/current liabilities position where the surplus had dropped by only £750.
(b) The reason for the fall is that stock now forms a much higher percentage of the current assets than it did in previous years. The bank would want to know why stock holdings are so high in relation to other assets – is stock being piled for good reasons (eg, you might have struck a good deal) or for bad reasons (eg, obsolete, unsaleable)?

5. Debtors

After scrutinising the current assets and current liabilities, the bank will then look more closely at three items from those figures: debtors, creditors and stock. First, debtors.

Any business which sells goods or services on credit will have a substantial sum of money tied up in debtors at any time. Obviously, you will not allow your customers a period of credit which is longer than is necessary to obtain, and then to keep, their custom. The last thing you should do is to put too much pressure on them to pay and consequently drive them into the eager arms of your competitors.

Banks are mindful of this and understand that some businesses have no choice but to grant long periods of credit. They calculate the period of credit given by a business by use of this formula:

$$\frac{\text{Debtors}}{\text{Annual Sales}} \times 365$$

This gives the period of credit in days. Banks know that this does not give an exactly true position. To do this they would have to use average debtors and average sales, and they do not usually go to this trouble. Let us have a look at a few examples and see how the bank might interpret the information.

Example 1

Year Before	Last Year	This Year
27 days	33 days	42 days

In this example, the period of credit given to customers is lengthening year by year. The alternatives which will flash through the banker's mind are:

(a) Is the business being progressively less efficient in the collection of its debts? Is insufficient attention being paid to this important aspect?

(b) Is there one (or more) long-outstanding debt which is distorting the overall picture and which, depending on the length of time outstanding, might be a bad or at least doubtful debt? This is the worrying one for the banker (and you).

(c) Are your customers in general simply taking longer to pay because of their own cash flow problems?

Of course, it might be none of these. It might simply be that you are having your arm twisted by your customers who are threatening to take their business elsewhere unless you give them more generous terms. Whatever the reason, the bank will want an explanation, and you would be advised to identify the cause before going to an interview with your bank manager.

Example 2

Year Before	Last Year	This Year
42 days	33 days	27 days

In this example we have the reverse position, where less time is being given to customers year by year. What are the alternatives here?

(a) More efficient collection of debts?

(b) You might be offering discounts to encourage your customers to pay more quickly.

(c) You might be putting a little pressure on your customers because you have a cash flow problem in your business.

(d) You might be making a higher percentage of cash sales as opposed to credit sales.

Unfortunately, bankers are a pessimistic lot by nature, and will invariably suspect that the reason is the most unfavourable one.

Example 3

Year Before	Last Year	This Year
33 days	27 days	42 days

In any situation where the pattern is inconsistent (as here) the banker will be unsure what conclusion to come to. Your explanation will be relied upon completely. In this particular example, the bank would be alarmed by the increase of 15 days following a decrease in the previous year, and the big fear would be that there is perhaps a long-outstanding debt distorting the figures, which could of course turn out to be a bad debt which will have to be written off.

Age list of debtors

Since a balance sheet is always several months out of date by the time the bank receive it, they will probably ask you for an up-to-date list of debtors outstanding, showing the date by which each debt is, or was, due to be paid.

Let us assume that your normal credit terms to customers are 30 days except for Company D, your biggest customer, which is 90 days. Today's date is 15 November and you produce the following list:

Customer	Amount	Invoice date	Due date for payment
	£		
Company A	827.43	5 Nov	5 Dec
Company B	1,233.96	7 July	7 Aug
"	946.29	26 July	26 Aug
Company C	602.40	29 Oct	29 Nov
Company D	5,460.22	8 Sept	8 Dec
"	6,496.26	5 Oct	5 Jan
"	7,242.87	2 Nov	2 Feb
Company E	3,406.90	12 Oct	12 Nov
Company F	1,143.65	22 Oct	22 Nov
	27,359.98		

There are two things which will cause the bank some concern. First, the amounts owing by Company B look like bad debts. Goods were sold to them on 7 and 26 July but both amounts remain unpaid. Obviously, you will have refused to do any more business with them until payment is received, and even if it is received eventually it would be unwise to supply them with any more goods.

The bank will want to know what steps have been taken to recover the debt and will ask for a realistic assessment of the chances of success. The bank will probably regard the total debt as bad and ask you to estimate the effect of having to write it off. Fortunately, while it is one of only six debtors, the amount is only about 8 per cent of total debtors.

In passing, the bank might also mention Company E, as payment from them is three days overdue, but this is not yet critical.

The second area of concern is Company D, which represents a massive 70 per cent of outstanding debts. The bank will be particularly concerned that this company is financially sound because, if their debt proves to be bad, the effect on the business would be disastrous. Perhaps you have been doing business with them for many years and you know they are good for their commitments, or maybe they are an undoubted multinational company, or maybe a Government department. Hopefully you will be able to reassure the bank of the safety of the debt.

Apart from the financial strength of Company D, the bank will also worry that you rely so heavily on one customer. While you might be excited about such a large contract, the bank will consider what would happen if Company D decided to take its business elsewhere. It would leave a huge gap in the sales turnover which would take a very long time to fill, if ever. Relying so heavily on this company also means that you are not going to be in a position to exert any sort of pressure on them, for fear of losing them. They are going to dictate terms to you.

A banker is always happier to see a company with a good, even spread of debtors and will always regard such a company as being much more soundly based than one for whom so much depends on one customer.

Now let us see what to make of the debtors of our three businesses.

Green Light Electrical Company Ltd

Last Year $$\frac{240{,}000}{2{,}350{,}000} \times 365 = 37 \text{ days}$$

This Year $$\frac{270{,}000}{2{,}450{,}000} \times 365 = 40 \text{ days}$$

This shows a consistent position. The slightly longer credit being given is insignificant. The bank would make no comment. They would probably still like to see a breakdown of debtors because these do represent a substantial asset, and the bank will want to satisfy themselves that all the debtors are safe.

Fire Tyres Ltd

Year Before $\frac{34,400}{165,000} \times 365 = 76$ days

Last Year $\frac{61,800}{322,000} \times 365 = 70$ days

This Year $\frac{20,700}{295,000} \times 365 = 25$ days

(a) Long credit given in the first two years, but collection is speeded up considerably in the latest year. The bank will need an explanation.
(b) The likeliest explanation, as stated previously, is that the company is probably doing more cash business by offering discounts.
(c) In view of the healthy state of the company, the bank are unlikely to want a breakdown of debtors.

AB Equipment

Year Before $\frac{22,500}{90,000} \times 365 = 91$ days

Last Year $\frac{24,750}{99,000} \times 365 = 91$ days

This Year $\frac{25,000}{108,000} \times 365 = 84$ days

(a) Long credit being given – three months.
(b) However, the terms are consistent over the three years, with a slight speeding up in the latest year.
(c) The bank will not be unduly worried. They may ask for a list because of the very long terms.

6. Creditors

Obviously, it makes good business sense to take as long to pay your creditors as they will allow, but the bank will want to see that you have the ability to pay without having to be pressurised.

The bank will use a similar formula to the one used for debtors to calculate the amount of credit your business is receiving from creditors:

$$\frac{\text{Creditors}}{\text{Purchases}} \times 365$$

This will give in days the period of credit which you are receiving. Again, it suffers from the same defects as the debtors calculation. Let us look at a few examples to see how a bank would view certain situations.

Example 1

Year Before	Last Year	This Year
30 days	38 days	48 days

The first thing to establish is the normal period of credit which you have agreed with your creditors. This will usually be 30 days – therefore the first year is spot on. In subsequent years, however, longer credit is being taken. Perhaps you have negotiated longer terms, but this is less likely than the possibility that you are taking longer to pay because of cash flow problems.

The bank are likely to ask you if you are experiencing pressure from any creditors to pay. It is common sense that if creditors are having to wait longer and longer for their money, they are going to get a little anxious about your ability to pay. The bank might ask you for a list of creditors, showing dates by which they should be paid (similar to the debtors list), to see if there is any substantial amount owing to one creditor, who might cause embarrassment to your business by demanding payment. If the total amount owing to creditors is evenly spread among them, then the position is not so critical.

Example 2

Year Before	Last Year	This Year
48 days	38 days	30 days

This shows that you are managing to pay your creditors more promptly each year, which could be because:

(a) Your business is thriving and cash flow is good, or
(b) You have been offered discounts for prompt payment which you are taking advantage of, or
(c) Your creditors are being much more strict with you, and not allowing you so long to pay.

Remember something said earlier – bankers are a pessimistic lot: they will think it is alternative (c).

Example 3

Year Before	Last Year	This Year
38 days	30 days	48 days

Again, this is the difficult one for the bank, as there is no trend. You will have to explain how you managed to achieve 30 days last year, but are taking 18 days longer this year. What has happened?

Preferential creditors

One question a banker will always ask in connection with creditors is, how much does the business owe to preferential creditors (eg, Inland Revenue, VAT)? Some balance sheets break down the creditors into trade creditors and preferential creditors, but most of them show a combined figure. Why is the question important to the bank? The word 'preferential' holds the answer.

Should the business go bankrupt (or into liquidation if it is a limited company), the preferential creditors will be paid in priority to the ordinary creditors. There might be little or nothing left to pay anything to the ordinary creditors. If the bank have lent money to your business and have not taken security, they will be an ordinary creditor. Even if the bank have taken security, they will probably still ask you the question, although the bank's position as a *secured* creditor cannot be threatened by the preferential creditors. (There is in fact one exception to this last statement, which we will discuss in Chapter 16 under the heading of Security.)

Let us turn once again to our three business. We do not have a figure for purchases, and therefore the sales figure will have to be used.

Green Light Electrical Company Ltd

Last Year $$\frac{400{,}000}{2{,}350{,}000} \times 365 = 62 \text{ days}$$

This Year $$\frac{450{,}000}{2{,}450{,}000} \times 365 = 67 \text{ days}$$

(a) The business is taking slightly longer to pay its creditors but the bank would not be too concerned about the extra five days.
(b) However, two months seems to be long, depending of course on the terms of trade agreed by the business with their creditors. The bank will ask what the terms are. If 30 days, then the bank will ask if creditors are putting on any pressure for payment, as invoices will be a month overdue before payment is made.
(c) The bank will want to know the amount of preferential creditors.

Fire Tyres Ltd

Year Before $$\frac{29{,}800}{165{,}000} \times 365 = 66 \text{ days}$$

Last Year $$\frac{55{,}000}{322{,}000} \times 365 = 62 \text{ days}$$

This Year $$\frac{52{,}000}{295{,}000} \times 365 = 64 \text{ days}$$

Consistent position over three years. The bank might mention that two months seems a little long. Terms of trade? Any pressure? It looks likely that the creditors are quite happy to wait two months for their money since that appears to be the position on a regular basis. The bank would be concerned only if the credit period shot up to two months from one month. There is nothing wrong with long credit terms provided the creditors are prepared to accept them. As far as you are concerned, the longer the better.

AB Equipment

Here we can use 'cost of sales' instead of 'sales'.

Year Before	$\frac{10,000}{45,000}$	× 365 = 81 days
Last Year	$\frac{12,000}{51,450}$	× 365 = 85 days
This Year	$\frac{14,000}{58,700}$	× 365 = 87 days

(a) Long credit being taken by this business, and the period is creeping up and up.

(b) In view of the overall length of time (the extra few days are not too important) the bank would want a list of creditors to see if there are any large individual ones who could cause problems if they demanded payment.

(c) The bank would also require a note of the amount of preferential creditors.

7. Stock

The bank will compare how quickly your stock is being turned over in each year. To maintain the correct level of stock is vital to any business – too little will affect the smooth running of the business, and too much means having cash tied up for longer than necessary.

The bank will use the following formula:

$$\frac{\text{Closing Stock}}{\text{Sales}} \times 365$$

This gives the number of days it takes for stock to turn over completely. Once again, it is not a formula which is going to give absolute accuracy, but at least it gives the bank an indication, when comparing one year with another, of whether the turnover is faster or slower. Unlike the debtors and creditors figures, which are taken from the company's books and should be accurate, this calculation depends entirely on the stock-take being accurate, which is an area where errors can be made. Obviously, any such errors will cause distortions.

The bank will expect a well run business to be turning over its stock with reasonable consistency – more or less the same number of days each year. If fluctuations are seen, the bank will want an explanation.

Example 1

Year Before	Last Year	This Year
42 days	46 days	65 days

The bank will want to know why, in the latest year, the stock is taking so much longer to turn over. The concern will be that, in that year, the stock figure contains stock which is obsolete and no longer saleable, thus distorting the figure upwards. The reason might be much simpler. It could be that just prior to balance sheet date there was a big delivery of stock, which will obviously inflate the figures.

Whatever the reason, it would be impressive if you had an answer ready for when your banker asks you the question.

Example 2

Year Before	Last Year	This Year
65 days	46 days	42 days

In the middle year, the stock turnover was speeded up and the improvement has been maintained in the latest year. The bank might ask how this has been achieved but it would be more in the nature of passing interest than a searching enquiry. The bank would be pleased with this situation.

However, it might not be as good as it looks. Just as in Example 1 the slowing down in the latest year could have been due to a delivery of stock just prior to balance sheet date, in this example, in respect of the middle and latest years, a delivery of stock might have been due at balance sheet date.

Example 3

Year Before	Last Year	This Year
46 days	65 days	42 days

The middle year is way out of line, and the bank will rely entirely on your explanation. The obvious answer is again a delivery, but when the 'odd' figure is flanked by figures which are similar to each other the chances of a faulty stock-take in the middle year are very high.

Consequences of errors in stock

In the figures in this last example, if the stock in the middle year was valued wrongly, it would be *over*valued, not *under*valued. If the closing stock is quoted at a figure higher than the actual figure, then this has the effect of showing a slower stock turnover. But the consequences are much more far-reaching than that.

If the closing stock is overvalued in the middle year, it has the effect of inflating the profits in that year, ie the profits would be overstated. However, the closing stock in the middle year becomes the opening stock in the following year and, if the opening stock is overvalued, it has the effect of understating the profits in that year. In other words, the gross profit in both years would be distorted.

Obsolete stock

As indicated earlier, the bank's major concern when they see a build-up of stock is that some of it might no longer be any good and will have to be written off. Obsolete or unsaleable stock will make the business look healthier on paper than it is in reality. The tell-tale sign of 'dead' stock is a slowing down of the stock turnover rate. If your balance sheet shows that situation, you will have to find the reasons for it.

A final point, before looking at our three businesses, is that if the stock figure is a combination of raw materials, partly finished goods and finished goods, the bank might ask for a detailed breakdown.

Green Light Electrical Company Ltd

Last Year $$\frac{420{,}000}{2{,}350{,}000} \times 365 = 65 \text{ days}$$

This Year $$\frac{460{,}000}{2{,}450{,}000} \times 365 = 68 \text{ days}$$

This shows a steady, consistent position. No need for comment or explanation. Levels of stock are rising in proportion to the increase in sales.

Fire Tyres Ltd

Year Before $$\frac{23{,}000}{165{,}000} \times 365 = 50 \text{ days}$$

Last year $$\frac{43{,}200}{322{,}000} \times 365 = 49 \text{ days}$$

This Year $$\frac{39{,}000}{295{,}000} \times 365 = 48 \text{ days}$$

Once again, this situation would raise no comment from the bank.

AB Equipment

Year Before $\frac{10{,}000}{90{,}000} \times 365 = 40$ days

Last Year $\frac{12{,}000}{99{,}000} \times 365 = 44$ days

This Year $\frac{20{,}000}{108{,}000} \times 365 = 67$ days

(a) This shows a build-up of stock in the latest year. Why? The bank will want an explanation.
(b) How is the stock made up? Raw materials or finished goods?
(c) If finished goods, why are they taking so long to sell? Are they still saleable?
(d) Is the stock-take in the latest year accurate?

8. Gross Profit

A comparison will be made of the gross profit over the past few years and an explanation will be needed if the trend is adverse. GP will be calculated as a percentage of sales:

$$\frac{\text{Gross Profit}}{\text{Sales}} \times 100$$

It is vital that a business makes as much GP as possible because it is from this that the overheads have to be deducted, many of which will be fixed costs, which have to be met irrespective of the amount of GP made. The bank would therefore be concerned to see any significant reduction in the GP percentage.

GP is the measure of how successful a business has been in its trading efforts. Expressed in its simplest form, it is the difference between the buying price and the selling price, and while that will be generally true for most wholesale and retail businesses, there is an added complication for manufacturing businesses.

Retailers and wholesalers

But first let us concentrate on businesses which buy and sell. Goods are bought at £20 each, marked up by £5 (ie 25 per cent), and sold at £25 each. The gross profit is £5 on each sale of £25, ie 20 per cent.

If the supplier increases prices from £20 to £21, then you will have to mark up by £5.25 to £26.25 (ie 25 per cent) in order to maintain your gross profit percentage of 20 per cent. In other words, if you continue to mark up your purchases by the same percentage, you will always maintain your gross margins. Incidentally, if you increase your sale price immediately, you will be selling for £26.25 some of the old stock which cost you £20 – a gross profit of £6.25 on £26.25, ie 23.8 per cent.

When calculating gross profit, adjustments are made for opening and closing stock in order to arrive at a figure for the cost of goods *actually* sold:

	£			£
Opening Stock	20,000		Sales	250,000
Purchases	210,000			
	230,000			
Less Closing Stock	30,000			
Cost of Goods Sold	200,000	(80%)		
Gross Profit	50,000	(20%)		
	250,000			250,000

Note that the cost of goods actually sold is 80 per cent of sales, and gross profit 20 per cent of sales.

For wholesale and retail businesses, the bank will expect to see a stable GP percentage because the costs are *variable* with sales. If the volume of sales falls, then fewer supplies have to be purchased, and therefore everything changes in the same proportions *so long as the mark-up remains at the same percentage.*

This can be illustrated by referring to our previous example. If the selling price is £25 per unit, then obviously 10,000 units have been sold if sales are £250,000. If the same stock had been purchased but only 9000 units had been sold, then sales and closing stock would have been:

(a) Sales 9000 × £25 = £225,000
(b) Closing stock – an extra £20,000 (ie 1000 units × £20), making £50,000 in all. The trading account would then read:

	£			£
Opening Stock	20,000		Sales	225,000
Purchases	210,000			
	230,000			
Less Closing Stock	50,000			
Cost of Goods Sold	180,000	(80%)		
Gross Profit	45,000	(20%)		
	225,000			225,000

Gross profit still represents a 25 per cent mark-up on cost of goods sold (COGS) and 20 per cent of sales. In other words, if you purchase goods and mark them up by a *consistent* percentage, then the gross profit as a percentage of the sales must remain the same. This is because the costs incurred before calculating gross profit are entirely *variable* with sales.

Competition

However, if you are in a business where competition is fierce, you might not be able to increase your selling price without losing business. If your supplier increases prices to £21 per unit, and you have no choice but to leave your selling price at £25, then you have the following situation, on a per unit basis:

	£	
Sales	25	
COGS	21	(84%)
GP	4	(16%)

Your gross margin has fallen from 20 to 16 per cent because you are unable to pass on the increase in costs to your customers. This is the major reason why the gross margin of any business falls, and the banks are well aware of this.

Diversification

The other thing which will affect GP percentage significantly is if you diversify into other goods, which attract a different mark-up.

Let us go back to the first example in this section where we had sales of £250,000 and gross profit of £50,000, and let us assume the following facts for the next year:

(a) You manage to increase sales to £275,000 with the same gross margin. Let us call these Goods (A).
(b) You diversify into Goods (B) which cost £10 per unit, and which you sell for £12 per unit.
(c) In respect of Goods (B), you buy 20,000 units and sell 18,000 units.

Goods (A)

	£			£
Opening Stock	30,000		Sales	275,000
Purchases	230,000			
	260,000			
Less Closing Stock	40,000			
COGS	220,000	(80%)		
Gross Profit	55,000	(20%)		
	275,000			275,000

Goods (B)

Opening Stock	Nil		Sales	216,000
Purchases	200,000			
	200,000			
Less Closing Stock	20,000			
COGS	180,000	(83.3%)		
Gross Profit	36,000	(16.7%)		
	216,000			216,000

However, the audited accounts will not show the split between Goods (A) and Goods (B), but will show total figures, as follows:

	£			£
Opening Stock	30,000		Sales	491,000
Purchases	430,000			
	460,000			
Less Closing Stock	60,000			
COGS	400,000	(81.5%)		
Gross Profit	91,000	(18.5%)		
	491,000			491,000

In this situation, GP percentage has fallen from 20 to 18.5 per cent simply because there is now a 'mix' of goods with different mark-ups. Of course, in many retail businesses there is a whole variety of goods being sold with different mark-ups, and a *significant* increase in the volume of sales of any one type of goods is going to affect the overall gross margin one way or the other, depending on whether that type of goods had a high or low mark-up in relation to the others.

Tactical pricing

Having said all this, however, the gross margin of a wholesaler or retailer should be fairly stable because the costs are variable. If you present the relevant information in a table it becomes clear what is happening:

	Year 1		Year 2	
	£		£	
Sales	100,000		200,000	
COGS	75,000	(75%)	160,000	(80%)
GP	25,000	(25%)	40,000	(20%)

If the selling price is £10 per unit in both years, then the buying price in Year 1 was £7.50 per unit, and in Year 2 was £8 per unit.

Obviously, you have not passed on the price increase which you have suffered, to your customers. As stated earlier, this might be because of competition, but the competition might work in your favour. You might have kept your selling price the same, knowing that your competitors were going to increase theirs. This has resulted in a big increase in the volume of sales (double) and gross profit of £40,000 as opposed to the previous year's £25,000. In other words, the lower gross margin is almost certainly the reason for the increase in business and the fatter gross profit.

So do not be defensive about a fall in margin. It can be a deliberate tactic to boost sales and therefore boost gross profit in money terms. The only cautionary note is that in order to 'carry' sales at the higher level, you are going to have to hold increased stocks, and if goods are sold on credit, then the debtors figure is going to be higher.

In other words, you are going to have much more money 'invested' in the business, which you might have to borrow. The interest on that borrowing is an overhead which will be deducted from the *net* profit, together with other overheads, which might have increased as a result of the increase in business.

Also, the money 'invested' in a business in order to run it, which is referred to as the capital employed, might be so much higher that the increased profit might represent a lower percentage of the capital employed. You, as proprietor, will be receiving a lower return on your money – but this is not a matter of prime concern to the bank and therefore outside the scope of this book.

Manufacturers

When calculating the gross profit of a manufacturing business, the costs of manufacture or production are deducted from sales. In addition to the cost of purchase of raw materials which is variable to sales, there are labour costs which businesses and their accountants regard also as variable costs, but which in reality are not entirely variable. For example, it is nearly always possible to achieve some increase in the level of production without either working overtime or taking on extra labour. But it is certainly easier to regard labour costs as being totally variable, and we shall do so in our examples.

Fixed and semi-fixed costs

There are some costs which do not vary at all, irrespective of the levels of production and sales. Such things as rent of the factory have to be paid whether the factory is working at full capacity or not. These are the *fixed* costs, which remain constant most of the time. For example, the rent of the factory might be reviewed every seven years, and therefore that cost will remain fixed for that period of time. When the rent is reviewed, that fixed cost will increase in that year, but then be constant again until the next review date. There are other fixed costs such as straight line depreciation of plant and machinery, ie the same amount of depreciation charged each year.

There are also semi-variable or semi-fixed costs, such as lighting and heating of the factory. For example, if you lose orders, which means that the factory works only four days instead of five, you can switch off the power on the fifth day, but the reduction in costs will not be exactly in proportion to the reduction in sales. However, a banker is never likely to want to be so precise, and therefore such costs can safely be included with the fixed costs.

The point is that the presence of fixed costs (remember that semi-fixed costs are included) will affect the gross profit margin, and therefore manufacturers with significant levels of fixed costs will never see the same stability in their GP percentage that wholesalers and retailers will see.

Example
A manufacturer has sales of £1 million and has variable costs of £650,000 (materials and labour), and fixed manufacturing costs of £150,000. Next year, sales increase by 50 per cent and variable costs move in the same proportion to sales. Look what happens to GP percentage:

	Year 1	*Year 2*		*Year 1*	*Year 2*
	£000	£000		£000	£000
Variable Costs	650 (65%)	975 (65%)	Sales	1,000	1,500
Fixed Costs	150 (15%)	150 (10%)			
Gross Profit	200 (20%)	375 (25%)			
	1,000	1,500		1,000	1,500

The GP percentage has risen from 20 to 25 per cent but there is no difference in the relationship between the variable costs of production (materials and labour) and sales. The increase has occurred because part of the manufacturing costs are fixed, and do not therefore increase when sales increase. Proportionately, they fall from 15 per cent of sales to 10 per cent of sales.

If it remains possible for the business to pass on into the sale price any increases in variable costs (ie increases in cost of raw materials, or wage rises), then a manufacturer's gross margin must increase as the volume of sales increases. Again, a table shows it clearly:

	£		£	
Sales	1,000,000		1,500,000	
Variable Costs	650,000	(65%)	975,000	(65%)
Fixed Costs	150,000	(15%)	150,000	(10%)
Gross Profit	200,000	(20%)	375,000	(25%)

It is obvious that as the volume of sales increases, the percentage of fixed costs to sales has to *fall*. Therefore, if variable costs can be maintained at a *constant* percentage of sales, gross profit percentage has to *rise*.

The situation will continue until such time as the level of fixed costs changes. If next year fixed costs doubled to £300,000, then sales would have to double, otherwise gross margin would fall. For GP percentage to remain at 25 per cent, fixed costs would not have to exceed 10 per cent of sales (assuming variable costs remained the same). If sales did double, the figures would be:

	£	
Sales	3,000,000	
Variable Costs	1,950,000	(65%)
Fixed Costs	300,000	(10%)
Gross Profit	750,000	(25%)

Remember that the extra complications in connection with the calculation of a manufacturer's gross margin relate only to production costs or factory costs. The rent of offices, the salaries of administrative staff etc will be regarded as overheads and be deducted from the profit and loss account.

Summary

Your bank will always want an explanation of any changes in gross margin, and it would be impressive if you could have the answers ready. A simple analysis, as already shown, would not only impress the bank manager, but would also be useful to you as proprietor of the business, as an indicator of what needs to be done to improve matters.

Just remember the main things which affect gross profit. For all businesses these are:

(a) Changes in the relationship between the cost of goods sold and the selling price charged to customers. If the mark-up percentage remains the same, then gross margin will be constant also.
(b) Mixing goods with different mark-ups. The introduction of a new 'line' of goods will cause this. Most businesses have a 'mix', and a significant increase in the sale of goods with a high gross margin will increase overall gross margins, and vice versa.

For manufacturers only they are:

(c) An element of fixed costs in the cost of production is always going to distort GP percentage. An increase in sales will increase gross margin, and vice versa.

As a final note, remember a point we made when discussing stock. If closing stock is incorrectly valued, then gross profit is going to be distorted, not only in that year but in the following year also. If closing stock is *undervalued* then gross profit in that year will be understated. The closing stock becomes the opening stock of the following year, and *undervalued* opening stock means that gross profit that year will be overstated.

Let us look at a few examples and how they might be viewed by the bank.

Example 1

Year Before	Last Year	This Year
21%	19%	14%

This is a serious reduction in GP performance, and an explanation would be sought by the bank.

The bank manager will be running through the options and you will have to provide the answer. If it is diversification, that is not too bad so long as it has resulted in larger gross profits in money terms. In fact, the business might now be much healthier because it is not relying on just one source for its profits. Also there might be scope for improving margins in future years.

Alternatively, it might be a big increase in fixed costs (if it is a manufacturing business) which has a drastic effect now but will improve in subsequent years as sales increase.

The most likely answer is that the business is having to pay more for its supplies, and is not passing on the increased cost to its customers. The selling prices need to be increased, but this might not be possible because of severe competition. It might be possible to obtain supplies more cheaply from a different source but failing that there is little that can be done.

One possible course of action would be to increase sales prices and to try to establish some sort of advantage for the product over that of competitors, eg the personal, friendly service of the local corner shop over the cut-price supermarkets. Failing that, the business will have to diversify.

If you find yourself in this latter situation, the bank will need to be convinced by your plans to get out of it.

Example 2

Year Before	Last Year	This Year
14%	19%	21%

This looks like a good progressive business: an excellent improvement in the middle year which has been maintained and built upon in the latest year, and while the improvement in the latest year is not as good as the improvement in the middle year, it would be unfair to expect it.

Example 3

Year Before	Last Year	This Year
19%	14%	21%

The bank would question the fall in performance in the middle year but would not be too concerned because the business has recovered in the latest year.

One possible explanation can be linked to our observations concerning stock turnover. If the closing stock in the middle year had been undervalued, this would deflate GP in that year. However, the undervalued closing stock of the middle year becomes the undervalued *opening* stock of the latest year which means that GP in the latest year would be inflated. Therefore, the GP performances of those two years might be much more even than the figures show.

Green Light Electrical Company Ltd

Last year $$\frac{162{,}000}{2{,}350{,}000} \times 100 = 6.9\%$$

This Year $$\frac{145{,}000}{2{,}450{,}000} \times 100 = 5.9\%$$

(a) A fall in GP of 1% – £17,000 less GP on an increased sales turnover. A serious position. Why?
(b) The directors will have to provide the answer, and I think we are now well aware of the options.
(c) If GP performance cannot be improved beyond 5.9 per cent, then sales would have to be increased to £2,745,000 in order to restore GP to £162,000. Can this be achieved?

Fire Tyres Ltd

Year Before $\frac{55,000}{165,000} \times 100 = 33\%$

Last Year $\frac{80,000}{322,000} \times 100 = 24.8\%$

This Year $\frac{115,000}{295,000} \times 100 = 39\%$

(a) A fall in GP percentage in the middle year. Why? Since sales doubled, it is probable that prices were kept deliberately low in order to achieve the increased volume of business.
(b) Margins have been vastly improved on a reduced sales turnover in the latest year. Having achieved the increase in volume, they have obviously restored their margins and, despite a fall in volume, they have achieved an increase in GP from £80,000 to £115,000.
(c) This business looks sound and streamlined now.

AB Equipment

Year Before $\frac{45,000}{90,000} \times 100 = 50\%$

Last Year $\frac{47,550}{99,000} \times 100 = 48\%$

This Year $\frac{49,300}{108,000} \times 100 = 45.6\%$

(a) Very high GP percentage but declining. Why? Partners will have to provide reason.
(b) Not much growth in the business – sales fairly static.

9. Net Profit

This aspect of a business is vitally important to a bank because it is from the retained profit that a bank usually has to look for repayment of any money lent to the business. There are exceptions where, for example, the bank is financing a specific project (eg property development) where repayment is going to come from the proceeds of that project.

Influences on net profit

We shall look at net profit again when we discuss the repayment of borrowing, but for the time being let us just concentrate on the things which affect net profit.

The first thing which affects it, of course, is the level of gross profit. If this falls then net profit is bound to fall also, because overheads still have to be paid, and most of them are fixed. Some will be variable, and a reduction in them will help to soften the blow, but it is highly unlikely that the level of NP can be maintained at a time when GP is falling.

The second thing is the overheads themselves. At a time when the level of GP is constant (or even rising), the level of NP can fall if there are big increases in overheads, especially the fixed costs such as the rent and rates of offices. The bank would want to look at the profit and loss account to see where the problem areas are, and will ask for your plans to rectify matters (assuming they are areas within your control).

It is pointless to look at NP in isolation because no real conclusions can be reached without taking GP into consideration.

Example 1

	Year Before	Last Year	This Year
	£	£	£
Sales	300,000	350,000	450,000
GP	63,000 (21%)	66,500 (19%)	63,000 (14%)
Less Overheads	30,000	33,000	36,500
NP	33,000 (11%)	33,500 (9.5%)	26,500 (5.9%)

The GP percentages are the ones used in Example 1 when we looked at gross profit. Here we can see that, although sales are increasing nicely, the business is not maintaining its gross margins. It is only because the business is managing to increase the actual volume of sales (ie new customers) that they are able to maintain the amount of GP; the margins are being squeezed. Despite the fact that the amount of GP is being maintained at just over £60,000, the amount of NP is falling because of the increases in overheads (an increase of around 10 per cent per year, which is not excessive).

Imagine the situation if no increase in the volume of sales had been achieved, ie sales had been £300,000 in each of the three years. In the latest year GP would have been £42,000 (14 per cent of £300,000) which, with overheads of £36,500, would have left an NP of only £5500 (1.8 per cent of sales).

If it is not possible for this business to restore gross margins, they will have to depend on an ever-increasing volume of sales and obviously, there is a limit to what can be achieved. The bank would be anxious because a levelling-off in sales would mean a fall in GP with a resultant fall in NP, which is the source of the bank's repayment.

So in this example we can see how a deterioration in the GP *performance* (ie a fall in the GP percentage to sales) can reduce the amount of net profit, even when the rise in overheads is not excessive. Impressive increases in the *volume* of sales can hide the problem for a time, but when increases in the volume start to level off, then the effect on NP will be considerable.

Example 2

	Year Before	Last Year	This Year
	£	£	£
Sales	300,000	350,000	450,000
GP	63,000 (21%)	73,500 (21%)	94,500 (21%)
Less Overheads	30,000	36,000	47,000
NP	33,000 (11%)	37,500 (10.7%)	47,500 (10.5%)

In this example, two things are different. First, overheads are increasing more heavily – by 20 per cent in the middle year and by 30 per cent in the latest year. Second, GP margins are being maintained on the increasing sales volume, which means that the effects of the increases in overheads are not felt. But the increases in overheads are there, and if there had been a fall in either GP performance or volume of sales, it would have had very serious consequences on net profit. If both had fallen then it would have been disastrous.

Let us imagine that sales had been £300,000 in each of the three years but GP had remained at 21 per cent, ie £63,000. Then the net profit in the middle year would have been £27,000 (9 per cent of sales) and in the latest year £16,000 (5.3 per cent of sales). Drastic reductions in NP would have occurred through a large increase in overheads and a lack of growth in sales.

Even if GP performance in the middle year had improved to 22 per cent, gross profit would then have been £66,000 but still, because overheads had increased by 20 per cent to £36,000, a net profit of only £30,000 would have been made, ie a fall of £3000 on the previous year. Obviously, in this situation, greater control needs to be exercised over those overheads which are capable of being controlled, and a big push needs to be made on sales.

In summary then, the bank will be looking in most cases at net profit as their source of repayment. As a result they will look closely at the relationship between sales, gross profit, overheads and net profit, and assess how changes in those relationships can affect the business's ability to repay bank borrowing.

Green Light Electrical Company Ltd

	Last Year	This Year
	£	£
Sales	2,350,000	2,450,000
GP	162,000 (6.9%)	145,000 (5.9%)
Overheads	157,000	155,000
NP	5,000 (0.2%)	(10,000) Loss

(a) Overheads are swallowing up gross profit. Small net profit made last year but net loss appears this year.
(b) In point of fact overheads in the latest year have been very well controlled. Although sales have increased by £100,000, overheads have actually reduced by £2000 – an excellent performance. Bank would be interested in how this was achieved.
(c) The trouble with this business is that insufficient gross profit is being made. Either sale prices have to be increased to restore gross margins, or the volume of sales has to be increased considerably – we calculated earlier that with a GP margin of 5.9 per cent, sales of £2,745,000 would have to be achieved in order to provide gross profit of £162,000 (the amount earned in the previous year).

(d) The bank would identify gross profit and not overheads as being the problem, and would ask to see proposals for improving it.

Fire Tyres Ltd

	Year Before	Last Year	This Year
	£	£	£
Sales	165,000	322,000	295,000
GP	55,000 (33%)	80,000 (24.8%)	115,000 (39%)
Overheads	51,400	72,600	97,700
NP	3,600 (2.2%)	7,400 (2.3%)	17,300 (5.9%)

(a) Sales doubled in the middle year, probably as a result of holding sales prices down, as reflected in the fall in GP percentage.
(b) Overheads increased by 41 per cent in the middle year which, together with the reduction in GP percentage, meant only a similar NP percentage to the previous year.
(c) The increase in overheads in the latest year is down to 34 per cent which, combined with the excellent GP performance, has resulted in a much improved net profit, both in amount and percentage.
(d) This business now looks very sound.

AB Equipment

	Year Before	Last Year	This Year
	£	£	£
Sales	90,000	99,000	108,000
GP	45,000 (50%)	47,550 (48%)	49,300 (45.6%)
Overheads	42,000	44,050	46,300
NP	3,000 (3.3%)	3,500 (3.5%)	3,000 (2.7%)

(a) A similar situation to Green Light: overheads swallowing up gross profit.
(b) Overheads increased by only 4.9 per cent in the middle year and by 5.1 per cent in the latest year. This represents good control.
(c) What is the cause of the poor net profit? Gross margins are declining but the real problem is the lack of growth in sales.
(d) This business needs a big sales push.

Summary of business profitability

It is so easy to become 'figure blind' and lose track of what is really important. Do the percentages really matter or is it the *amount* of profit which should be concentrated on? Which is better:

(a) Net profit of £10,000 on sales of £100,000 (10%)? or
(b) Net profit of £20,000 on sales of £500,000 (4%)?

If a business had achieved (a) last year and (b) this year, would that represent progress or not? After all, it is the money that matters, not the percentage. We return again to *your* return on the capital employed in the business. The investment in assets required to support the much higher level of activity will reduce your return. You might get more by investing that capital on the stock market, in a building society or a bank. While you might have doubled the net profit, you might be better selling the business and investing elsewhere.

The crunch comes if sales start to fall and those extra assets you needed become redundant, eg you might have rented or bought extra factory space, office space, extra labour, salesmen, office staff, computer systems. What happens to all of that?

The monetary value of profit is important, obviously, but you should not have a total disregard for the margins. Every business must try to increase its profits in order to survive – indeed, a static business is a deteriorating one – but the rate of growth must be gradual if you are going to be around a long time. There are a lot of businesses which 'go like a bomb' for a time but they tend to disappear just as quickly as they arrived. It is easy to be tempted by big contracts with low margins, but why should you work for nothing?

Remember: *your* return on *your* capital is *your* concern. The banks merely earn a rate of interest on money which they lend to you, irrespective of whether you are doing well or doing badly. No matter how much interest they might show in your activities, and while they genuinely want you to prosper, their priority is always going to be to make sure they get *their* money back.

10. Summary

We have now examined all the various aspects of a balance sheet which a banker would examine, but each has been looked at in isolation.

We need to look now at the overall picture and see how some of them sometimes overlap. To a certain extent we have seen this already where two indicators seem to point to the same conclusion.

Let us look at our three businesses, making notes as a banker would.

Green Light Electrical Company Ltd

Net worth

Reduced from £280,000 to £250,000 (including directors' loans).

Profit and loss account reduced £10,000 – loss!

Why have directors' loans reduced? Any plans for further reductions?

When were premises last valued? Possible hidden reserve.

Current assets

A reduction in net current assets from £150,000 to £120,000 (excluding directors' loans from current liabilities).

Why has position deteriorated?

Have fixed assets been purchased? If not, then potential further losses.

Acid test

Position worsened from (£270,000) to (£340,000).

What plans do directors have for improving situation?

Debtors

Days' credit being given: 37, 40.

Consistent position.

Substantial asset. Are they all good? List required.

Creditors
Days' credit being taken: 62, 67.
Reasonably consistent.
What are terms of trade? Two months seems a little long.
Any pressure as a result?
Amount of preferential creditors?

Stock
Stock turnover days: 65, 68.
Constant position – looks OK.

Profit

	£	£
Sales	2.35 m	2.45 m
GP	162,000 (6.9%)	145,000 (5.9%)
Overheads	157,000	155,000
NP	5,000 (0.2%)	(10,000) Loss

Very poor NP turning to net loss.
Overheads not the problem. They have reduced although sales increased.
Gross profit is the problem.
GP percentage fell. Why? Competition? Can prices be increased?
Can volume of sales be increased? Sales rose by only 4.25 per cent in latest year.
Directors' proposals required.

Summary of balance sheets
Poor profitability – net loss now appeared.
Directors pulling out their money. Sign of trouble?
Question directors closely.

Management figures
Net current assets fallen from £120,000 in June to £60,000 in March. Is this a loss of £60,000 in nine months?
Situation very serious.
What are directors doing about it? The slide must be stopped.
Urgent meeting required.
What security is held? Bank may have to demand repayment of borrowing unless directors have convincing plans.

Fire Tyres Ltd

Net worth
£25,300, £32,000, £48,300 – good progress.
Good profits being made and retained in business.
Possible hidden reserve.

Current assets
Surpluses increasing – £2800, £10,500, £17,000.
Strong position.
No tax 'Last Year'. Why?
Substantial improvement in cash position.

Acid test
Deficits of (£20,200), (£32,700), (£22,000).
What happened in middle year? Must have something to do with doubling sales turnover.
When stock is included trend is consistent (see current assets above).

Debtors
Days' credit being given: 76, 70, 25.
Tremendous speeding up of debtor collections in latest year. Why?
More cash sales? Discounts being offered? This could explain improvement in cash position.

Creditors
Days' credit being taken: 66, 62, 64.
A little long – two months. What are terms of trade?
Consistent position – therefore probably no problem.

Stock
Stock turnover days: 50, 49, 48.
Constant position. No comment.

Profit

	£	£	£
Sales	165,000	322,000	295,000
GP	55,000 (33%)	80,000 (24.8%)	115,000 (39%)
Overheads	51,400	72,600	97,700
NP	3,600 (2.2%)	7,400 (2.3%)	17,300 (5.9%)

Sales doubled in middle year – gross margins fell – deliberate policy?
Sales trimmed in latest year – gross margins improved.
Excellent profit performance in latest year.
All looks well.

Summary
Looks a sound, well run business.
Looks like effort was made to boost volume of business in middle year at expense of margins and, once achieved, business has been streamlined in latest year with margins restored.

AB Equipment

Net worth
£36,000, £39,500, £42,500 – unexciting progress.
Small increases in profits.

Current assets
Surpluses £19,500, £25,750, £25,000.
Slight reduction in latest year. Why?
Probably due to investment in fixed assets after previous year's low investment.

Acid test
Surpluses £7500, £11,250, £2000.
Big reduction in latest year.
The apparent reason is that stock now accounts for a higher proportion of current assets than previous years. Why is this? Overstocked?

Debtors
Days' credit being given: 91, 91, 84.
Long terms. Is this unavoidable?
Any potential bad debts since term is so long?
List required.

Creditors
Days' credit being taken: 81, 85, 87.
Nearly three months. This is long. What are terms of trade?
Any pressure due to length of term? Possibly not, because term is consistent over the three years although term is getting slightly longer.

What is amount due to preferential creditors?
Term more or less matches term for debtors which will ease the cash flow position.

Stock
Stock turnover days: 40, 44, 67.
Build-up of stock in latest year. Ties in with observation on acid test.
Why is there a build-up? What is it a build-up of? Raw materials or finished goods? Any unsaleable stock?

Profit

	£	£	£
Sales	90,000	99,000	108,000
GP	45,000 (50%)	47,550 (48%)	49,300 (45.6%)
Overheads	42,000	44,050	46,300
NP	3,000 (3.3%)	3,500 (3.5%)	3,000 (2.7%)

Good gross margins but declining, and GP being swallowed up by overheads.
Can overheads be trimmed? Increased by only 4.9 per cent in middle year and by 5.1 per cent in latest year. It will be difficult to make any improvements in that area.
Volume of sales is insufficient. Increased by only 10 per cent in middle year and 9 per cent in latest year. What can partners do about this?

Summary
Progress slow and sluggish. Looks reasonably sound, but sleepy.

Part 2

The Bank's Approach to Lending Propositions

11. Introduction

As mentioned in the Introduction to this book, each business is different and will receive individual treatment when the bank are trying to decide whether or not to lend to that business. However, there are certain principles which can be applied to all businesses and the bank will adopt the same *general* approach to all propositions put to them to lend money.

There are five basic questions the bank will ask:

What is the money needed for?
How much is needed?
How is it going to be repaid?
When will it be repaid?
What security can the bank have?

This is not the full story, of course. There are lots of other things which will affect the bank's decision to lend or not, for example, your past record, your trustworthiness, how long you have had an account, what sort of customer you have been, your business ability, how valuable you are as a customer.

It is this common approach to lending situations which we shall examine in this part of the book. Once again we shall use our three businesses as examples to illustrate the various points.

First of all, we need to fill in some details of what the businesses do, their history etc, to which we will refer from time to time.

Green Light Electrical Company Ltd

This company has had an account at the same branch for 20 years. It operates an electrical wholesaling business and the two directors each hold 50 per cent of the shares.

In the past two years, trading has been difficult. Last year they agreed to reduce their remuneration slightly but, despite this gesture, a small loss was made – the first in the company's history.

Just over nine months ago the bank agreed to increase the

company's overdraft from £150,000 to £175,000 because the company was finding it a little difficult at times to operate within the limit of £150,000. As security the bank hold a debenture (more about this when we discuss Security in Chapter 16, but suffice to say at this point that a debenture means that all the company's assets are available to the bank as security). The freehold land and buildings were valued recently at £75,000.

As a condition of increasing the lending, the bank insisted that quarterly management figures were produced.

The directors now find that an overdraft limit of £175,000 is not really sufficient, and ask for an increase to £200,000.

Fire Tyres Ltd

Jack and his son Charles are the only directors of Fire Tyres Ltd, a company formed by Jack just over 15 years ago to sell new and remoulded tyres. Progress has been fairly modest but the freehold property owned by the company is now worth £40,000. The company has banked at the same branch for seven years.

The company has an overdraft limit of £25,000 and has given the bank a debenture as security. Jack and Charles have also each given guarantees of £25,000. The company finds that it can operate easily within the overdraft limit.

The directors make an appointment to see their bank manager. A service garage in the town has become vacant following the death of the former proprietor four months ago. The asking price is £60,000, made up as follows:

£50,000 for the freehold site
£10,000 for plant and equipment.

The equipment is in good condition. They intend Charles to run the garage while Jack continues to run their existing business.

The directors ask the bank to lend the company £55,000 to purchase the garage, in addition to the existing overdraft of £25,000. They are prepared to offer the garage as extra security.

AB Equipment

This business has three partners, all in their early 50s, and the partnership has banked at the same branch for 12 years.

Their business is the production of specialist equipment for hospitals and they manufacture in anticipation of long-standing orders from Government departments. The business operates from rented premises and shares the building with another company which occupies a smaller, self-contained section of the building.

An opportunity has now arisen to purchase the freehold of the whole building for £120,000. After the purchase, renovations costing £10,000 will need to be carried out and then the smaller section will be sold to the other business which occupies the building, at a cost of £50,000. It is thought that the renovation work will take three months to complete.

The partners have raised personal finance of £30,000 which they will inject into the business. They have raised this finance by increasing the mortgages on their private homes.

They ask the bank to lend the balance of £100,000, which will reduce to £50,000 when the sale of the smaller section has taken place.

The remaining £50,000 will be repaid over a period of 10 years. The partnership operates without overdraft.

12. What is the Money Needed For?

Banks will lend for almost anything so long as it is legal. Many customers do not understand why a bank want to know what they intend to do with the money, and find it offensive and unnecessarily prying. When lending to a business, the bank want to be sure that the money is going to be used in the business beneficially, and preferably to create increased profits.

Banks are always happy to be approached to lend money to finance a profitable new contract, but not all approaches are for that purpose. It might be the exact opposite. The business might be losing money and finance is needed to keep the company going on a day-to-day basis.

This is the situation with Green Light Electrical Company Ltd. We have seen from the figures that losses are being made and that is why they are finding it so difficult to work within their overdraft limit. They are not generating money themselves (ie profits) and therefore need more and more from the bank.

In such situations the bank have to be convinced that the losses are temporary and that the business will soon return to profitable trading. The bank must have confidence in the directors' ability to do this.

In Green Light's case, the bank would do all they could to help. They have been customers for 20 years and the latest year saw their first ever loss. The bank will explore all avenues before demanding repayment – but if a demand has to be made, they will make it.

Banks are not the complete ogres which many businessmen think them. They would not pull the rug out from under its feet the first time a business runs into trouble. The bank will try to help the business 'trade through' the problem, provided there is a reasonable chance of success.

The two major purposes for which a bank is approached to provide finance are (a) working capital, ie financing day-to-day operations, and (b) purchase of fixed assets.

Working capital

This is provided by means of an overdraft. You agree with your bank a limit up to which your current account can be overdrawn, and you must operate within this limit, otherwise the bank have the right to refuse to pay your cheques.

If you always received money owed *to* you before you had to pay money owed *by* you, there would never be a need for an overdraft. This is perfect business timing. However, when the timing is different and you need money which you do not have, you need an overdraft to smooth out these timing differences.

A business with cash sales should have less need of an overdraft than a business which has to sell on credit, although the problem of selling on credit can be eased by arranging longer credit terms with your suppliers (if possible) than you give to your customers.

The maximum period for an overdraft is 12 months, at which time you will have to discuss with your bank whether the overdraft limit can be reduced or cancelled. More often than not, businesses try to negotiate a higher overdraft limit for the next 12 months, and the bank will readily agree provided the reasons are good, namely extra finance needed to support a greater volume of business, resulting ideally (but unfortunately not necessarily) in greater profits.

Purchase of fixed assets

Requests to borrow to purchase fixed assets will receive a mixed response. If the purchase is machinery which is more modern and efficient and which will increase productivity, the bank will see such a proposition as being beneficial to the business, maybe not immediately but certainly in the medium term.

The purchase of vehicles which are essential to the smooth, efficient running of the business (vans for distribution, for example) will be regarded more highly than the purchase of directors' cars.

If you operate your business from leased or rented premises, you might have the opportunity to purchase the freehold. It is understandable that you would want to take advantage of this chance because it would make your balance sheet look much stronger, and of course any future appreciation in value would then belong to the business.

Such a purpose does not increase profits, however. Indeed, it might reduce them because the business would have to meet loan repayments and interest. Rent would no longer be payable of course, and this saving will offset some of the cost of borrowing.

The request from one of our businesses, AB Equipment, is to purchase the freehold of its premises: a perfectly acceptable proposition provided the cost of borrowing can be met from *existing* profits. This is the snag. Lending to finance a new sales contract will generate *extra* profit which can be used to repay the borrowing, but not so when lending to buy premises.

Our other business 'guinea pig', Fire Tyres Ltd, wanted to borrow to purchase a garage site. The bank in that case would want to see audited accounts of the garage to ensure that it had been making profits up to the previous owner's death. The bank would want to be certain that the garage could generate sufficient profit to repay the bank borrowing.

This is a good purpose because it is going to increase the existing profits of Fire Tyres Ltd (provided the accounts show this to be the case).

Evidence

Whatever the purpose of an advance, the bank will always want to see evidence to support anything you say. If you are having any building work done, extensions or repairs for example, you will have to produce estimates of the costs involved, usually two estimates. If planning permission is needed for what you intend to do, the bank will want to see that you have it before they will agree to lend to you.

Perhaps you want the bank to finance the performance of a big new contract which you have just obtained, or maybe some new project which you are about to start. The bank would want to see details of your costings to ensure that you have not underestimated them, and would have to be satisfied that the new undertaking was going to be profitable.

Usually you will have to provide a cash flow forecast to support any request for an overdraft (more about this when we discuss how much is required).

Do not get upset! It is not that the bank are doubting your honesty and integrity, but merely carrying out their duty of ensuring that any money they lend is lent wisely and safely.

Impress by saving time

It is wise to anticipate what the bank will want to see, and by taking the necessary evidence with you into the interview, you will not only save time but also impress the bank that you have 'done your homework'.

Most requests to borrow money involve two meetings – the first when the businessman outlines the proposition, only to be told by the bank that they want to see various papers to support what is being said, and the second (some time later) when the businessman has the necessary information. It is so much better for all concerned if you can short-cut the proceedings by having the evidence with you at the first meeting.

Examples
In the case of Green Light, who want to increase their overdraft limit to £200,000, the bank would want to see a cash flow forecast to be sure that £200,000 was going to be enough. The last thing the bank want is to agree a figure, only to find that three months later they are being approached again for yet another increase because the original requirements were underestimated.

As regards AB Equipment, who want to borrow £100,000 to buy the freehold of their existing premises, the bank would want to see a professional valuation to ensure that the premises were worth that amount. The business also intends to spend £10,000 on renovations to the property. The bank would want to see two estimates to show that the figures are realistic.

Fire Tyres want to purchase a garage site. Once again a professional valuation will be needed and the bank would also want to see audited accounts for the garage business to verify that the business is viable.

Memorandum of Association and Articles of Association

These documents apply only to limited companies. When the bank open an account for a limited company, they always ask to see copies of the company's Memorandum and Articles, which they will keep in their files. The contents of these documents become very important when the bank are considering lending to the company.

The business activities in which a company may engage are clearly stated in the Memorandum. If the bank lend to a company for a business activity which is *not* stated in the Memorandum, then the lending is void. This means that the bank will not be able legally to enforce repayment of the money against the company. The company could not be sued for a debt which is void.

Obviously, therefore, the bank need to look closely at the Memorandum to ensure that the purpose for which a company is borrowing is one of the business activities stated in the company's Memorandum.

Examples

AB Equipment want to borrow to buy their premises, and if the business had been a limited company, the bank would inspect the Memorandum of Association to ensure that the company had power to do this. However, AB Equipment is a partnership, and such businesses do not have a Memorandum and Articles of Association.

Fire Tyres Ltd want to borrow to buy a garage, which is a completely different type of activity from selling tyres. Obviously, the two activities are closely related (if you want to buy tyres you would not go to a grocer's shop) but there is a difference. If the bank are going to lend around £50,000 for the purchase of the garage business, they would not take any chances. If the Memorandum does not specifically cover the operating of a garage, then the bank would insist that this activity be included in the Memorandum before they would agree to lend.

With Green Light, the bank are being asked only to increase the existing overdraft limit, and therefore the question of the *purpose* of the borrowing should have been considered when the overdraft was first agreed.

Incidentally, in the case of Green Light, the bank would need to look at the Memorandum in respect of the *amount* being borrowed, but not in respect of the purpose. We will consider this and other aspects concerning the amount required, in the following pages.

13. How Much is Needed?

In the previous chapter, when we were discussing the various purposes for which a bank might be asked to lend, it seemed appropriate to mention the sort of evidence which would be required in respect of each purpose.

However, the need for that evidence is more relevant when the bank are considering the *amount* that is being asked for. The bank will need to verify that the amount is realistic. Is it too much? Is it too little? How have you arrived at that figure?

If you need £7000, it is pointless asking for £5000 simply because you think the bank will lend £5000 but not £7000. The bank might agree £5000 only to find you going over that figure. This causes friction between you and your bank. It is much better to ask for £7000 in the first place, and risk being rejected.

Fixed assets

In respect of the purchase of fixed assets, there should be no problem in verifying the amount needed. For example, if you wish to purchase property, you get a professional valuation and submit it to the bank who, if your application is successful, agree to lend you the money on loan account, which you repay over a period of time by monthly instalments.

Working capital

The evidence connected with a request for an overdraft to assist with day-to-day finance of the business is not quite so simple. The bank will want to see a cash flow forecast. This is a forecast of the inflow and outflow of cash in your business over the next 12 months, and of *when* it is likely to occur. The period can be for less than 12 months but never for more than that. You will be asked to provide such a forecast on a month-by-month basis, and you might need assistance from your accountant or even your bank manager.

In this way, it should be possible to calculate what the

maximum level of overdraft is likely to be, and when it is likely to be needed. Obviously this will occur when your outflows are very high and your inflows very low. Your bank will have special forms which you can fill in.

Details for the forecast

In order to construct a cash flow forecast, you have to make assumptions and estimates of the business's income and expenditure over the next 12 months, when that income will be received, and when that expenditure has to be made. Let us make a few estimates:

Sales

(a) Projected sales for the next 12 months will be £390,000.

(b) Credit terms are one month, ie the income from sales will be received in the month after the sales are made.

(c) The sales in the month before the forecast starts were £25,000.

(d) The sales for the next 12 months are expected to occur as follows:

Months 1–3	25,000 per month
Months 4–6	30,000 per month
Months 7–9	35,000 per month
Months 10–12	40,000 per month

Purchases

(a) Projected purchases for the next 12 months will be £330,000.

(b) Credit terms are one month, ie payment will be made in the month following the purchases.

(c) The purchases in the month before the forecast starts were £21,000.

(d) The purchases for the next 12 months are expected to occur as follows:

Months 1–3	21,000 per month
Months 4–6	25,000 per month
Months 7–9	30,000 per month
Months 10–12	34,000 per month

Note. Both sales and purchases will be affected by the fact that the factory closes down for two weeks in August. Therefore the figures for September will be affected.

Salaries (a) These are £2000 per month.
(b) They are to be reviewed in month 10.
(c) It is expected that they will be increased by 10 per cent in months 11 and 12, ie £2200 per month.

Rent (a) Annual rent is £10,000.
(b) It is payable by four equal instalments of £2500 in February, May, August and November.

Rates (a) Annual rates are £4000.
(b) They are payable in two equal instalments of £2000 in January and July.

Electricity (a) Estimated at £2700 for the year.
(b) Payable £600 in March, £600 in June, £700 in September, £800 in December.

Gas (a) Estimated at £1700 for the year.
(b) Payable £500 in January, £500 in April. £400 in July, £300 in October.

Telephone (a) Estimated at £800 for the year.
(b) Payable £200 in February, May, August and November.

Of course, there are many other items of expenditure, such as stationery, postage, advertising and so on, but to avoid obscuring the point, we will not clutter up the example with too many items.

Compiling the forecast

We can now plot the income and expenditure on the cash flow forecast. Let us assume that it is now December and therefore we are going to produce a forecast of cash requirements for January to the following December. Let us further assume that the balance of the bank account at the beginning of our period, brought forward, is £6000 overdrawn, which is shown as (6.0) on line (B). All other minus figures will be shown in brackets also.

We are going to work on full calendar months but it is possible to pick any date in the month to start; for example, you could work from the 15th of the month to the 15th of each following month. It is quite a good idea to start from the date in the first month when your cash position is at its worst.

You will note the following points from the completed cash flow forecast on page 79:

(a) Because one month's credit is both given and received, sales and purchases appear in the forecast in the month after they occur.
(b) Therefore the sales and purchases figures shown in the first month, January, relate to the previous month, that is the month prior to the start of the forecast.
(c) By the same token, the projected sales and purchases for the twelfth month (ie *next* December – £40,000 and £34,000 respectively), will not appear in our cash flow forecast. They will be the first items of the *next* forecast.
(d) The reduction in the figures for sales and purchases in September reflects the fact that the business closed down for two weeks in August for the annual holidays.
(e) Cash balances have improved by £11,400 in the year. We started £6000 overdrawn and we have finished up £5400 in credit.

Limitations of cash flow forecasts

The bank will look along line (F) to see what the maximum overdrawn balance will be during the next 12 months. We can see that it occurs in February – £7200. Therefore the business needs an overdraft limit of at least £7200, but in reality it will probably need much more than this because of the weaknesses of such a forecast:

(a) The figures are estimates only, and therefore a contingency has to be built in for variations – say 10 per cent on all the figures shown, although it is probably wiser to allow more. A 10 per cent contingency would add £720 to the maximum overdrawn balance of £7200, meaning that an overdraft limit of at least £8000 is needed.
(b) The forecast works on *net* figures between income and expen-

Example of a cash flow forecast

(A) Month	Jan	Feb	Mar	Apr	May	Jun	Jul	Aug	Sep	Oct	Nov	Dec
(B) Opening bank balance	(6.0)	(6.5)	(7.2)	(5.8)	(4.3)	(4.0)	(1.6)	(1.0)	(0.7)	(1.4)	1.3	2.4
Income												
Sales	25.0	25.0	25.0	25.0	30.0	30.0	30.0	35.0	17.0	35.0	40.0	40.0
(C) Total income	25.0	25.0	25.0	25.0	30.0	30.0	30.0	35.0	17.0	35.0	40.0	40.0
Expenditure												
Purchases	21.0	21.0	21.0	21.0	25.0	25.0	25.0	30.0	15.0	30.0	34.0	34.0
Salaries	2.0	2.0	2.0	2.0	2.0	2.0	2.0	2.0	2.0	2.0	2.2	2.2
Rent		2.5			2.5			2.5			2.5	
Rates	2.0						2.0					
Electricity			0.6			0.6			0.7			0.8
Gas	0.5			0.5			0.4			0.3		
Phone		0.2			0.2			0.2			0.2	
(D) Total expenditure	25.5	25.7	23.6	23.5	29.7	27.6	29.4	34.7	17.7	32.3	38.9	37.0
(E) Cash increase (decrease)	(0.5)	(0.7)	1.4	1.5	0.3	2.4	0.6	0.3	(0.7)	2.7	1.1	3.0
(F) Closing bank balance	(6.5)	(7.2)	(5.8)	(4.3)	(4.0)	(1.6)	(1.0)	(0.7)	(1.4)	1.3	2.4	5.4

diture and then only on the balance at the *end* of each month. Therefore an overdrawn balance of £7200 at the end of February will be the maximum figure seen, but only if income comes in before expenditure goes out. In reality a much higher overdrawn balance might be seen *during* the month of February.

Let us suppose for a moment that the rent in February is due on the 1st of the month, and that during the first week of the month, a payment of £5000 has to be made to suppliers. If none of the income for February has been received by that time, then we shall see an overdrawn balance of £14,000:

£	
6,500	overdrawn balance at the beginning of February
2,500	payment of rent
5,000	payment to suppliers
14,000	

The position might be improved if the business has the option of delaying payment to the suppliers until some payment is received from customers, but there is a limit to which this can be carried before the suppliers start applying a little pressure.

(c) Any money owed by customers, receipt of which is seriously delayed, or indeed any money owed which turns out to be a bad debt, will have a serious effect on the forecast. A bad debt of £5000 will worsen the projection by that amount for the rest of the period. That is one reason why banks ask for a list of debtors because they are well aware of the effect of delayed or non-receipt of money owing to a business.

A business which produces this cash flow forecast might ask for an overdraft limit of £7500 or maybe £10,000, but even at £10,000 they will find that, many times during the year, the overdrawn balance is right up to, and sometimes in excess of, the limit. This is because of the weaknesses inherent in such a forecast. With a forecast like this, the business should be asking for an overdraft limit of at least £15,000, or even £20,000.

The point is that you are doing yourself no favours by asking for too little. Provided that repayment and security considerations are satisfactory, the bank will prefer to grant an overdraft facility of £20,000, within which your business can comfortably operate, rather than £10,000 which you are constantly exceeding.

Why produce forecasts with such weaknesses?

The whole idea of a cash flow forecast is that the bank knows you have given the matter some thought and not just picked a figure out of the air. It is never going to work out exactly – how can it? Apart from the obvious shortcomings already discussed, who can predict accurately 12 months in advance? However, the bank will expect the 'actual' figures to bear *some* resemblance to the projected ones.

Our cash flow forecast shows the business operating without overdraft by the end of the period in question. We have omitted, of course, a number of expenditure items which would affect that position, but in reality it is common to see cash flow forecasts showing similar situations. Sometimes quite substantial credit balances are projected.

Somehow it never seems to work out that way in reality!

Another point about the forecast in our example is that it reflects a business with evenly distributed sales throughout the year. There are, of course, many businesses with heavy seasonal sales (holiday hotels, for example) and this will have to be reflected in the forecast. Such a business could well have surplus cash at certain times of the year, and a need for overdraft at others.

Amount related to net worth

Let us cast our minds back to when we were looking at the net worth of a business. We said that the bank are highly unlikely to lend more than a business is worth; indeed, they will expect to lend a good deal less.

Once the bank are satisfied that the amount being asked for is realistic, their next step is to compare that amount with the net worth of the business. The bank's view is that you, the proprietor of the business, should have a bigger stake in the business than the bank have. If the bank are lending more than net worth then it is the bank who have the major stake.

There are exceptions to this rule, but not many. The bank might be persuaded to exceed net worth if the excess is going to be temporary and will be cleared from some identifiable source, eg sale of a property or investment, or the raising of a mortgage.

Failing that, you will be wasting your time asking for more than net worth, and your only way forward then is to contribute more yourself.

Green Light Electrical Company Ltd

This company wants to increase its overdraft to £200,000 because it is losing money and cannot operate within its existing limit of £175,000. The net worth as at last balance sheet date was £250,000 if directors' loans were included, and £220,000 if not included. Whichever figure is used, it has reduced from the previous year, and an amount of £200,000 would be generous in comparison. The bank would be almost matching net worth.

However, something else has to be remembered. The management figures for the nine months after balance sheet date show further losses being made, which will reduce the net worth even more. The bank could now have the bigger stake if they agreed to increase the lending to £200,000. Against this gloom, the freehold land and buildings have recently been valued at £75,000 but are shown in the balance sheet at £60,000. This hidden reserve will increase the net worth by £15,000.

Nevertheless, the relationship betwen the bank's stake and the proprietors' is not one which the bank will view favourably. On the plus side, the company has banked with them for 20 years and until recently has been successful. The bank will be as helpful as possible, but with the best will in the world, unless the directors can show definite proof of their ability to stem the tide, the bank will not want to lend any more to this business.

Fire Tyres Ltd

This company has an overdraft limit of £25,000 and wants to borrow a further £55,000 to buy a garage – making £80,000 in all.

As at last balance sheet date, the net worth was £48,300, but their existing premises, which are shown in the balance sheet at £6,900, are now worth £40,000 – a hidden reserve of £33,100. This boosts the net worth to £81,400.

Lending of £80,000 is extremely generous against this net worth, but the company has shown its ability to make profits, and provided the bank are satisfied that the new business will contribute to increased profitability, then they would not be too unhappy with the relationship.

AB Equipment

This business has no borrowing at the moment but wants to borrow £100,000 in order to buy and renovate the premises from which it operates, and then in four months' time, part of the property will be sold off for £50,000.

The net worth of this business in the most recent balance sheet is £42,500. There are no hidden reserves but the partners have raised £30,000 of personal finance which they will have to inject into the business, in the form of either capital or loans. Either way, it increases the net worth to £72,500.

To lend £100,000 is obviously too generous, but £50,000 will be temporary – four months only. In this situation, the bank might well be prepared to lend in excess of net worth because the relationship between the stakes would correct itself very quickly.

It should be mentioned here, as a reminder, that we are merely comparing the relative amounts. The ultimate decision whether or not to lend will depend very much on the repayment proposals and the security available.

Memorandum of Association and Articles of Association

The final point about amount concerns once again an inspection of the Memorandum and Articles, but only if the business is a limited company.

The Memorandum might place a limit on the amount that the *company* can legally borrow. Any borrowing in excess of this limit would be void, which means that the bank could not enforce repayment of it. The Articles might place a limit on the amount that the *directors* are permitted to borrow on behalf of the company.

It is important to the bank that these limits, if present, are observed.

14. How is it Going to Be Repaid?

Banks are not charities, and any money they lend, they expect to be repaid. Indeed, they will never lend at all unless they are reasonably confident that the business is capable of repaying it.

But where does repayment come from, and what amount has to be repaid? Let us tackle the second question first.

How much has to be repaid?

A banker will try to calculate the *annual* cost of borrowing a certain amount of money and then assess whether the business can meet that cost. Borrowing is done by means of either overdraft or loan, and the cost will depend on which method is used. Not that you will have any choice – broadly speaking, overdrafts are for day-to-day working capital purposes, and loans for the purchase of fixed assets.

Overdraft

Let us assume that you want an overdraft of £50,000 and you have produced a cash flow forecast which shows that you can operate within that limit. The forecast should give the bank some idea of how heavily the overdraft is going to be used, and this will allow them to calculate roughly how much interest will be charged.

The bank will charge interest at (say) 3 per cent over the bank's Base Rate which for the sake of argument we shall put at 10 per cent – so the bank will charge at 13 per cent. A rough calculation of interest can then be made for the coming 12 months, based on what looks like being the *average* overdrawn balance for the whole period. It is then a matter of simple arithmetic:

Average overdrawn balance £20,000 at 13% = £2600 interest
Average overdrawn balance £30,000 at 13% = £3900 interest
Average overdrawn balance £40,000 at 13% = £5200 interest

Of course, a number of things might happen to distort the figures. Base Rate is almost certain to change a few times during the year, and therefore the rate of interest charged by the bank will change also. The 3 per cent margin over Base Rate will remain constant. Therefore, if Base Rate rises to 11 per cent, you will be charged interest at 14 per cent.

Something might occur which makes your cash flow forecast inaccurate, and while originally an average overdrawn balance of £30,000 looked likely, £40,000 now looks more realistic. This might be due to the fact that because of competition you are having to give longer periods of credit to your customers than you originally anticipated, or perhaps you are doing a greater than expected volume of business, which is requiring extra finance.

The bank is aware of these possibilities, and all they are trying to do before agreeing to lend is to get a rough idea of what it is going to cost your business to service the overdraft.

It is the interest, and the interest only, which represents the cost of an overdraft – there is no programme for the repayment of the overdraft itself. Remember that the purpose of an overdraft is to smooth out *temporary* shortages of cash caused by (perhaps) late receipt of money from a customer. Once the money is received from the customer, the need for the overdraft should disappear. Obviously, it is not this simple but that is why there is no repayment programme – it is not meant to be for an extended period.

The other theory is that, as the business prospers and makes greater and greater profits, then there will be more and more internally produced money to finance the day-to-day activities, and therefore less need for borrowing. In other words, the overdraft will repay itself as the need for it diminishes. In practice it does not work like this because you are always trying to increase sales and expand the business, which creates *new* needs for the overdraft as the expansion has to be financed.

Permanent overdrafts?

So how does an overdraft get repaid? The simple answer is that it doesn't! The bank will insist that the situation is reviewed at least once a year, when you will be asked how you see the coming 12 months developing, and what level of overdraft you will need from the bank.

The bank might be quite happy to renew the overdraft year after year provided that the business is prospering and making sufficient profits to cover the interest, *and* so long as they believe that the business is capable of repaying the actual amount of the overdraft, if it becomes necessary. The only time the bank will demand repayment of the overdraft itself is when it looks as if the business is getting into serious difficulties and is likely to go 'bust'. Of course, at a time like that, the business might be totally incapable of repaying the overdraft, and it is for this reason that the banks take security at the time of lending.

To a large extent, therefore, many businesses have 'permanent' overdrafts – but it would be wrong for you to think of an overdraft in this way, for two reasons. First, it is reviewed at least once a year, and the bank can refuse to renew, if they wish. Second, the overdraft is repayable on demand, that is you have to repay the lot immediately if the bank demand that you do so. Having said this however, there is no reason why a *successful* business should not be able to be overdrawn permanently, and renew every year.

Loans

A loan has a repayment programme over a number of years, and the monthly instalments will repay both the capital sum and the interest. The loan reduces gradually and the interest is calculated on the amount outstanding. This means that the interest in the early years will be very high but it will reduce as the amount of the loan outstanding reduces.

Imagine that your business needed a loan of £50,000, to be repaid over ten years. The capital repayments would be £5000 per year but the interest would be much higher in the early years than later. It is the wrong way round for the business, which will hopefully be in a much stronger position in the *later* years, and much more capable of carrying the heavier burden than at the outset.

What the bank do, however, is to equalise the burden of the interest over the whole ten-year period, so that the business pays the same amount each year. This will then be divided by 12, which gives the amount the business must pay each month for 120 months, to repay both capital and interest. The bank have interest tables which allow them to calculate how much will be required each month to repay any amount over any period at any interest rate.

Rough calculation

Before asking for the loan, you might like to calculate *approximately* how much it is going to cost you. Assume a loan of £50,000 over ten years at 13 per cent. Calculate the interest on the halfway figure, ie £25,000 (this is the equalising effect). Interest on £25,000 at 13 per cent is £3250 *per year*. Therefore total interest will be £3250 × 10 = £32,500. Add to this the capital amount of the loan, £50,000, and you will arrive at the total you have to repay: £82,500. The loan is over ten years and therefore your repayments will be £8250 per year or £687.50 per month (say £700).

As mentioned briefly already, the calculation of the interest on the halfway figure has equalised the burden of the interest over the whole ten-year period. However, remember that this will give only an approximation of the cost – your bank will be able to give an exact figure. The exact figure will be greater than your approximate figure because you will have used simple interest, whereas in reality the interest will be compounded: interest will be charged on interest also.

The bank's Base Rate will change many times over a ten-year period but usually no allowance is made for this in calculations. Who can predict when it is going to change, which way (up or down), or by how much? There are going to be both rises and falls, which will probably cancel each other out. If you want to be pessimistic, add another 1 per cent to the interest rate, ie 14 per cent. The annual repayment figure will then be £8500 and the monthly repayment figure £708.33. You can see that a round figure of £700 is not going to be far wrong.

A final word on the burden of a loan in the early years. Most banks nowadays offer special schemes which can be adapted to meet the needs of each individual business. For example, you might be able to arrange that during the first year or two, you pay interest only, with no capital repayments. All banks offer something different – so just ask!

Where does repayment come from?

When the bank have calculated the annual cost of the borrowing, they will then want to know where the money is coming from to cover this cost. There are two sources.

Specific identifiable source

The bank borrowing might be of a temporary nature until an asset is sold (eg property or investment) or until some more permanent finance is raised, eg mortgage on premises.

On a longer time-scale, the bank might be asked to finance a specific contract or project which is going to generate the necessary funds to repay the bank borrowing. Building projects will fall into this category, where the bank finance the construction, and are repaid when the development is sold.

Normal profits

The usual source of repayment for most businesses is the profits from trading. The bank will want to see that the business has a good past record of both making profits and keeping those profits in the business, but they have been criticised for placing too much emphasis on what has gone before, and not enough on what is going to happen. It has been said that the use the business intends to make of the money and the effect it has on the business, are much more important than past history.

There is much to be said for this argument, and banks have had to adapt their rather conservative attitude. They will now ask for projections of sales and profits, but they will treat what they receive with some caution. Anyone can produce projections which look good – indeed, nobody is going to present a pessimistic projection when trying to persuade the bank to lend. At least, what has happened in previous years is *fact*; projections tend to be fiction!

The extent to which the bank will rely on the projections depends a good deal on who has drawn them up. If the bank regard the directors as prudent and trustworthy, they will treat their projections much more seriously than those provided by people for whom the bank have less regard. If the business's financial adviser has been involved in the preparation, the bank will feel more confident in the figures.

In any case, the bank will still regard previous performances as a reliable base. For example, if a business has increased sales by an average of 10 per cent for each of the last three years, the bank will not take too seriously a projection which shows a sales increase of 25 per cent. It might be possible, but the directors would have to be very persuasive to get the bank to believe it.

So, bankers look at profits in two ways when trying to assess whether or not a business is capable of servicing any borrowing. They look back at what has happened, and in some cases, though not all, they will ask for a projection of what is to come.

The need for a projection will depend on circumstances. Let us assume that your business already has an overdraft limit of £50,000, and you are having the annual review of that limit with the bank. The following are three possible examples of the net profit shown in your accounts for the last three years.

Example 1

Year Before	Last Year	This Year
£4,000	£7,500	£10,000

Your net profit is increasing each year, and remember that interest on the overdraft will already have been deducted from the profit figure. In other words, you are demonstrating that your business can easily service the overdraft (remember that the bank will only want interest to be covered on an overdraft). If you are asking your bank to renew the overdraft for the next 12 months at the same figure of £50,000, it is unlikely in the circumstances that the bank will need to see a projection of profits before agreeing to the renewal.

Example 2

Year Before	Last Year	This Year
£10,000	£7,500	£4,000

Although you are still managing to make a net profit *after* the bank's interest has been deducted, the amount of profit is reducing. The bank would be wondering how soon losses would start to appear, and they would question the safety of the amount of the overdraft itself.

In this situation, if you asked the bank to renew at £50,000, the bank *would* want a projection to see whether profits are going to reduce further, or whether recovery is round the corner.

Example 3

Year Before	Last Year	This Year
£4,000	£7,500	£10,000

Here we have the same figures as in Example 1 but this time let us assume that you are asking the bank to increase the overdraft limit from £50,000 to £100,000 because you intend to increase the volume of business. In this situation, you are asking for *new* borrowing, and therefore the bank will want to see a projection to ensure that the business is capable of servicing the *extra* borrowing.

The projection

The one thing you must not do is try to fool the bank with projections which are too optimistic. Make them realistic. If you are going to err, then err on the side of caution.

1. Sales

Your first task is to estimate the likely level of sales in the next 12 months (the bank will not want a projection further than that). As stated earlier, if your usual increase in sales is around 10 per cent, then the bank are going to be wary of any estimate in excess of 10 per cent. Of course, there might be good reason for estimating more than 10 per cent, eg you might recently have won a new contract. If that is the case, it must be built into the projection because you can justify the increase.

2. Gross profit

The next thing to do is estimate the gross profit percentage which you feel can be achieved on those sales – remember that this should be fairly stable for nearly all businesses but especially for non-manufacturing ones. Once again, the bank will be guided by past margins as to how seriously they take your projection.

Let us assume that the following figures represent your results for the last two years and your projection for the coming year:

	Last Year	This Year	Projection
	£	£	£
Sales	300,000	330,000	365,000
GP	60,000 (20%)	66,000 (20%)	91,000 (25%)

In respect of sales, the projection looks realistic. An increase of 10 per cent was seen 'This Year' over 'Last Year', and you are projecting around 10 per cent again. However, gross profit has been steady at 20 per cent but you are now projecting 25 per cent because you intend to increase your selling price.

The bank would question how certain you were that you could achieve sales of £365,000 if you increased your prices. You might lose business to your competitors, and unless you can justify your optimism, the bank might insist on a more modest projection of expected sales at the increased price.

3. Overheads

Overheads need to be projected next, and this will be a difficult thing to do because there can be no uniform increase for each item. The most reasonable thing to do is to increase each item by the same percentage as it increased this year, and maybe build on a further contingency of (say) 5 per cent. Some items will not need to be increased at all; for example if you rent your premises and a rent review is not due in the next 12 months, you can use the same figure as was paid this year. If a review is due and you do not know the new figure, it is probably prudent to increase the amount actually paid by 50 per cent.

When overheads have been deducted from gross profit, you will be left with your projected net profit. It is probably better to leave bank interest out of your projected overheads, and then the bank can see whether you will be making sufficient net profit to cover interest (and capital repayments if you have borrowed by way of a loan).

There is no hope whatsoever of your projections being absolutely right, but so long as the estimates are reasonable, the bank will be impressed that you have done them without being asked. The bank will probably modify the figures to look at the worst possible position, but provided that your figures are not outrageous, they will probably go along with you.

What might the bank expect by way of projections from our three businesses?

Green Light Electrical Company Ltd

This company made a net profit of £5000 'Last Year' and a net loss of £10,000 'This Year'. We have seen from management figures that further losses seem to have been made since the last balance sheet date.

Therefore, we have a loss-making company with an overdraft limit of £175,000, asking for the limit to be increased to £200,000. This will involve extra interest *and* the bank will be doubtful about the safety of the money they have already lent. It is vital that Green Light returns to profitability as soon as possible.

Let us look again at this company's performance:

	Last Year		This Year	
	£		£	
Sales	2,350,000		2,450,000	
GP	162,000	(6.9%)	145,000	(5.9%)
Overheads	157,000		155,000	
NP	5,000	(0.2%)	(10,000)	Loss

(a) What sort of projection could this business produce in order for the bank to support it further? Remarkably, overheads were reduced from £157,000 to £155,000 but it would be prudent to build in an increase in the projection. Is anything going to occur in the next 12 months which will result in a big increase in overheads, eg an increase in fixed costs? The business will have to inspect each item closely and if nothing exceptional is due to occur, then build in an increase of (say) 10 per cent – ie overheads will be (say) £170,000.

(b) The business is making losses and therefore it would probably be wise to look no further than a break-even point. It needs to make a gross profit of £170,000 in order to cover projected overheads. If it has a gross margin of 5.9 per cent again, then that means that sales will have to be £2,881,300 in order to give a gross profit of £170,000. If Green Light can achieve a gross margin of 7 per cent, then sales of £2,428,600 will produce a gross profit of £170,000.

(c) Green Light's directors must decide what needs to be done. If it is not possible to achieve gross margins better than 5.9 per cent, then sales have to increase from £2,450,000 to £2,881,300 – an increase of 17.6 per cent. Is this increase possible? Sales increased 'This Year' from £2,350,000 to £2,450,000 –an increase of only 4.25 per cent. Therefore the bank would be very sceptical about a sales projection showing a 17.6 per cent increase.

(d) It would appear that Green Light's best course of action would be to increase sales prices in order to produce a gross margin of 7 per cent. This means that they would break even with a slight *fall* in sales from £2,450,000 to £2,428,600. If sales of the previous year could be matched (£2,450,000), the gross profit on a margin of 7 per cent would be £171,500.

(e) The big question is, of course, could the same sales be achieved when prices have been increased? And if they could, the company would still only just have bettered break-even. But that would be better than a loss, and maybe they could build on that in the following year.

The bank would probably be prepared to accept the following projection with accompanying comments, as being realistic:

	£
Sales	2,450,000
GP	171,500 (7%)
Overheads	170,000
NP	1,500

(a) We intend to restore gross margins to 7 per cent.
(b) Because of that we feel it might be too optimistic to project sales beyond the figure achieved 'This Year'.
(c) We have increased overheads by 10 per cent. We managed to reduce them 'This Year', and therefore we are confident that we can contain them to 10 per cent.

This is a projection done by sensible people, and the bank is much more likely to support the company than if a projection had been produced showing sales of (say) £3,000,000 with gross profit £210,000 (7 per cent) and net profit £40,000. Such a projection would be saying that selling prices were going to be increased *and* sales would increase by £550,000 – an increase of over 22 per cent compared with the increase of only 4.25 per cent achieved 'This Year' on the old prices.

Occasionally perhaps, such performances might occur but the bank would prefer to see a little less ambition. A too-optimistic forecast in this company's situation might destroy any confidence the bank had in the directors' ability to turn the company round. The bank would be looking for a more realistic programme of recovery.

Fire Tyres Ltd

You will recall that this business is doing quite well. It runs a tyre sales outlet and has an overdraft limit of £25,000. They now want to borrow an extra £55,000 to buy a garage. Let us remind ourselves of their trading performance:

	Year Before	Last Year	This Year
	£	£	£
Sales	165,000	322,000	295,000
GP	55,000 (33%)	80,000 (24.8%)	115,000 (39%)
Overheads	51,400	72,600	97,700
NP	3,600 (2.2%)	7,400 (2.3%)	17,300 (5.9%)

The bank would probably be looking at a loan over ten years at (say) 13 per cent, which would mean annual repayments of around £9000 to £10,000 to cover capital and interest.

The profits of the new business would be the expected source of repayment of the loan, and the bank would want to see the audited accounts of the garage for the last two or three years, to see if sufficient profits had been made to cover the cost of the borrowing. The bank would also want to see projections of how the directors saw the garage performing under their control. This would not be an easy matter because it is a new venture and not quite the same line of business as their existing one, and because of this the bank would view such projections rather critically.

In the circumstances, the bank would probably ask for a projection of their existing business as well, because if things go wrong with the garage, the profits of the existing business would be the source of repayment. A net profit of £17,300 was made in the latest year (remember, interest on the existing overdraft will already have been deducted from the net profit) and therefore this figure is more than adequate to cover the annual cost of the new borrowing, ie £10,000 maximum.

However, the latest net profit represented a vastly improved performance on the previous year, and therefore the bank will want to be sure that this was not just a 'one-off'. If the directors can assure the bank that this level can be maintained, and perhaps even improved upon, the bank will have no doubts about their ability to service the borrowing.

The projection which would be produced would depend on what the directors' policy was for the next 12 months. In the middle year, they doubled sales at the expense of gross margins. In the latest year, they restored the margins at the slight expense of sales.

(a) So what might they project? Well, overheads in the latest year went up from £72,600 to £97,700 – an increase of 34 per cent. Each item will have to be inspected to see if that increase contained any exceptional items which will not be repeated in the coming year, or whether the coming year will involve items which were not encountered 'This Year'. In the absence of any exceptions, it would appear prudent to estimate a 40 per cent increase in overheads. This would give projected overheads of £136,000.
(b) If a net profit of (say) £20,000 is to be achieved (a modest increase), then a gross profit of £156,000 has to be made.

Assuming that the gross margin of 39 per cent can be maintained, then that means sales will have to be £400,000 – an increase of 26.25 per cent on 'This Year'. Can this be achieved? Alternatively, if the directors feel that gross margins can be increased to 45 per cent, then sales of £345,000 need to be made – an increase of 17 per cent. How confident are they that sales could reach that figure with increased sale prices?

Two possible projections might therefore be:

	1	2
	£	£
Sales	400,000	345,000
GP	156,000 (39%)	156,000 (45%)
Overheads	136,000	136,000
NP	20,000 (5%)	20,000 (5.8%)

The directors could probably convince the bank that either of these projections is feasible because their past record is good. If the new business looks viable, the bank would be happy with the repayment prospects.

AB Equipment

This business appears to be a little sluggish. It manufactures hospital equipment, ordered by Government departments. They have no borrowing at the moment but want to borrow £100,000 in order to buy and renovate the premises which they presently rent. Part of the premises will then be sold to existing tenants in four months' time for £50,000. The remaining £50,000 will be repaid over ten years.

Their trading performance has been:

	Year Before	Last Year	This Year
	£	£	£
Sales	90,000	99,000	108,000
GP	45,000 (50%)	47,550 (48%)	49,300 (45.6%)
Overheads	42,000	44,050	46,300
NP	3,000 (3.3%)	3,500 (3.5%)	3,000 (2.7%)

A loan of £50,000 over ten years at (say) 13 per cent would mean annual repayments of around £9000 to cover capital and interest. There is also a 'one-off' interest payment of around £2000 on the other £50,000 which will be outstanding for four months; but let us ignore this – the bank's concern will be the term loan of £50,000.

We can see that the business is making a net profit in the region of £3000 per annum which is inadequate to cover the cost of the borrowing. However, the rent payment would no longer be relevant once the freehold was purchased, so this amount would be available. The profit available for repayment would therefore be £3000 (net profit) + £1500 (rent) = £4500.

It is still not enough, and the bank would want a projection to see if the coming year was going to generate the required level of profit.

(a) Overheads 'This Year' increased from £44,050 to £46,300 – a rise of 5.1 per cent. Deduct rent of £1500 which would no longer be payable if the bank agreed to lend, and we have £44,800. Inspect other overheads for any unusual items, but in the absence of them, estimate an increase of (say) 10 per cent. Therefore projected overheads would be £44,800 + 10 per cent = £49,300 (say £50,000 in round figures).

(b) If the business is to achieve a net profit of £10,000 in order to cover the cost of the borrowing, then with overheads of £50,000 it means that a gross profit of £60,000 has to be made. If the gross margin remains around 45 per cent, then sales of £133,000 have to be achieved.

	£
Sales	133,000
GP	60,000 (45.1%)
Overheads	50,000
NP	10,000 (7.5%)

This is an increase in sales of £25,000 on the latest year's figure of £108,000 – an increase of just over 23 per cent. Can this be achieved? The increase in sales in previous years has been:

£90,000	to	£99,000 (10%)
£99,000	to	£108,000 (9%)

(c) It looks highly unlikely. Remember also that such a performance would only generate sufficient profit to cover the cost of borrowing. Unfortunately, the purpose of the borrowing is not going to add to the profits. If the purpose had been to finance some lucrative new contract, then *new* profits would have been generated. But the purchase of premises is not going to do that.

(d) Unless the partners have some revolutionary new plans, it looks as though this business is not going to be able to meet the cost of borrowing. Since they make specialist equipment and their customers are Government departments, they are unlikely to be able to increase their selling price in order to increase their gross margins. Indeed, the fall seen in gross margins suggests that they are having to absorb increases in costs of production already.

Depreciation

Before we leave the subject of profit available to cover the cost of borrowing, it is necessary to mention depreciation. You have to remember that depreciation is deducted from profits but it does not represent money going out of the business. It is only a book entry. Therefore, when a bank are looking at the net profit figure of a business, that figure will have had depreciation deducted from it. The bank will add back depreciation to the net profit to arrive at a new figure of profit available to service bank borrowing.

Summary of points about projections

The subject of projections is a little more complicated than other aspects of this book, and it would be useful to summarise what has been said.

You will recall that I said that the usual way to approach the preparation of a projection is to estimate first sales, then gross margin, then overheads. This is the textbook method and the one which optimistic (usually over-optimistic) businessmen will adopt.

You will have noticed that I approached it a little differently, as your bank will:

(a) I estimated overheads and then built on a figure for net profit – as far as the bank are concerned this must be the minimum figure to cover the cost of the borrowing, but in your case it will probably be the figure you would like to see for net profit (being realistic).

(b) You then know how much gross profit you need to make, and by applying the expected gross margin, you arrive at the sales figure needed to make it all happen.

(c) You are then in a position to know whether this can be achieved, and if it cannot, what needs to be done.

This seems to be a much more responsible way of going about it than picking out of the air some fanciful figure for sales which you hope, rather than think, you can achieve, and then making everything else fit in with it. Businessmen have to be optimistic, but that optimism must not be allowed to run riot.

Alternative projections

Above all, be honest. You must not be tempted to underestimate overheads or overestimate the gross margin or sales you might achieve. It is not a bad idea to project figures which you think are realistic, and then prepare one or more other projections to see the effect on your business if you have got it wrong.

For example, if your realistic projection shows a 20 per cent rise in overheads and a gross margin of 15 per cent, see what will happen if overheads rise by 30 or 40 per cent, and gross margin is only 12 or 10 per cent. It is useful if you know what your 'downside' is, ie your worst possible position, and you might even consider what you would do in that situation. The good businessman is the one who is rarely surprised, and who has a contingency plan for most situations.

Remember that projections are based only on estimates and therefore can never be completely accurate. So having more than one projection makes sense. Your bank will not ask you for more than one, but they could not fail to be impressed if they could see that you had taken into account the effects of not achieving your realistic targets.

Need to monitor progress

Preparing the projection is only half the story. Not only will it assist your bank in deciding whether to lend, but it can be an invaluable management aid to you. You must not forget about it. You must continually monitor actual results to see if you are achieving your projections. Don't wait until the audited accounts are prepared after the year-end, because it will be too late then.

If you draw up a profit report every quarter and you discover you are not on target, you know about it early enough to do something about it. If your bookkeeping is up to date, it should not be too difficult to produce the report. The only time-consuming thing would be the stock-take. But it is your business, your capital, your livelihood. It would be time well spent.

I promise you one thing. If you send your bank a quarterly profit report (with comparisons to the projections) together with management figures (debtors, creditors, stock), your banker will be speechless with admiration. The bank's confidence in you as a businessman will rocket. And that can't be bad!

Repayment review

The bank calculate the cost of borrowing and then assess whether or not the business is capable of covering it.

(a) *Overdraft*. The cost of borrowing is the *interest only* but the bank will need to be satisfied of the business's ability to repay the *amount* of the overdraft, if necessary. The bank will probably take security as a precaution. An overdraft has to be reviewed at least once a year.

(b) *Loan*. The cost of borrowing is the interest *and* the capital amount over a fixed period of years.

(c) Occasionally there will be a specific source of funds, eg proceeds of a specific contract which bank lending is financing, but in nearly all cases the usual source of repayment is the profits from normal trading. The bank will want to see that the business has a good track record in respect of profitability, and will often ask for projections of future profits.

15. When Will it Be Repaid?

Traditionally, banks have always been short-term lenders. Indeed, overdrafts are repayable on demand. If the bank tell you to repay your overdraft, you have to do so without delay.

Ironically, the bank are likely to demand repayment when you are least able to do so. They are not going to ask for their money to be repaid if the business is buoyant and profitable. Demand will be made when the business is making losses, with no hope of recovery. It is in those situations that the bank have to rely on their security in order to recover their money. So, if you have a good, profitable business, don't worry when you receive a letter from the bank! It will not be a demand for repayment.

Loans are granted on the basis that they will be repaid over a certain number of years. Anything up to 20 years would be considered by the bank, although they will want to keep the period as short as possible.

Loans will probably be subject to more formal documentation than overdrafts, with the conditions under which the loan is granted being clearly stated. One thing which will be stipulated is the conditions under which the total amount of the loan becomes immediately repayable. These may vary slightly from bank to bank, but by and large a bank is unlikely to demand repayment of a loan unless the repayment instalments are in arrears.

The term of a loan will be strongly governed by the business's ability to repay. A five-year loan might be requested, but when the bank calculate the cost of borrowing (interest and capital), it might be found that business profits are not sufficient to achieve repayment over a five-year period.

This does not mean that the proposition will be declined. The bank will look at whether a longer period would be more suitable (say ten years). This would place less strain on annual profits by reducing the annual cost of repayment. If those profits were sufficient to meet the cost of borrowing over the longer period, and provided the bank were happy with the other aspects of the proposition, then it is feasible that they might restructure the loan in this way.

Banks are flexible on the length of time over which they are prepared to lend. A long-term loan will never be declined solely because of the period. There will be other factors (eg uncertain profitability, inadequate security etc) which will be the real reasons for the rejection.

16. What Security Can Be Given?

The need to provide security probably worries customers most about borrowing from a bank. What will the bank want? Will there be enough? Will they sell it? These are the questions which run through a borrower's mind and I will try to answer them, but first. . . .

Why is security taken?

Banks take security in case something goes wrong with the repayment plans. A bank would not lend in the first place if there were doubts about the business's ability to repay, no matter how much security was available. But though repayment might look feasible at the time of lending, many things can happen to change that.

It is in these situations that the bank turn to their security in order to obtain repayment of money lent. It is a second line of defence, a cushion to fall back on if the business is in a loss-making situation, with little or no chance of recovery.

Banks do feel a sense of responsibility in pointing out to customers when they think it would be unwise for the customer to borrow and to give personal assets as security. For example, when a customer wants to buy a business, and maybe give the family home as security, if the bank think that the business is not really viable, they will not lend, although the lending would be fully secured by the house.

What will the bank want?

There are three main types of security which a bank will take: life policies, shares in companies quoted on the Stock Exchange, and property (houses, factories). If the business owns its premises, then the bank will prefer to take this as security rather than your own *personal* assets.

The bank will also be prepared to take a guarantee from someone else to cover the amount of lending. If you are the sole proprietor of your business, there will never be a need for *you* to give a guarantee, as you are already fully liable for the business debts. Similarly, a partner is liable for the debts of the partnership, and therefore will not need to give a guarantee.

If you are a director of a limited company, however, you are not legally liable for the company's debts. This is because a limited company is recognised by the law as having an identity of its own, completely separate from that of the directors or shareholders. This is why a lot of business people want to go limited because they will not then be personally liable for the company's debts.

But the bank will not let you escape. If the bank lend to the company, they will take a guarantee from the directors. This makes the directors *personally* liable for the company's debts, but since a guarantee is only a promise to pay, the bank might ask the directors to back up their promise with tangible security, such as life policies, shares, or their houses.

Banks always like to have guarantees by the directors because they are a demonstration of their personal commitment to the company, but the guarantees can sometimes be dispensed with if the company itself owns sufficient assets, which can be charged as security for borrowing.

A special type of security given by a limited company is called a debenture, and this will be discussed later.

How much security will the bank want?

The value of the security must cover the amount borrowed. A lot will depend on the type of security given, so let us look at each type and imagine that the customer wants to borrow £10,000.

Life policies

The security value of a life policy is the *surrender* value, ie the amount which the insurance company would pay now, in exchange for the surrender of the policy. It is not the amount which is payable at maturity – that might be many years in the future.

If you are 40 years old, and you took out a £50,000 life policy 15 years ago, which is due to mature in 20 years' time when you are 60, the policy will not be worth £50,000 until maturity date. If the policy is 'with profits' then it could be worth considerably more than £50,000 on maturity. But now, when you are wanting to borrow £10,000 from your bank, the value of the policy will depend upon the amount of premiums you have paid, and the bonuses, if any, which have been added to the policy by the insurance company. The bank will write to the insurance company to find out what the present surrender value is.

The bank might be prepared to lend an amount equal to the surrender value because the surrender value is unlikely to decrease. Indeed, it will continue to increase provided you continue to pay the premiums. Life policies are the most stable form of security, and while banks prefer to see a safety margin between the surrender value and the amount lent, they will be more generous in the amount they are prepared to lend than they would be with any other type of security.

In our example, therefore, provided that the surrender value of the policy is no less than £10,000, the bank will probably regard the security position as being satisfactory, but remember, they prefer to have a margin.

Shares

Usually the bank will only be interested in shares in companies which are quoted on the Stock Exchange. Shares in private companies will not be attractive as security because it will be difficult for the bank to value them accurately, and even more difficult to sell them, should this be necessary.

The value of public company shares can easily be found by reference to newspapers, but because share prices can fluctuate so much, the bank will want a significant margin between the present value of the shares and the amount they are being asked to lend. In any case, they will be much less generous than if a life policy is the security.

As a rough guide, you should be thinking in terms of double cover – in our example where the proposed borrowing is £10,000, the bank would be looking for £20,000-worth of shares. They might be a little more generous if the shares were well spread over several companies rather than just in a few, because then the risk is less.

Property

Quite often the only asset of any real value that customers can offer as security is their house. Values of residential property generally rise, and while in some exceptional circumstances they can fall, the trend is usually upwards.

The value of your house for security purposes is the difference between market value and the amount outstanding on your mortgage – unless you are one of the fortunate few who have paid off your mortgage. If your house is worth £60,000 and the mortgage is £30,000, that leaves £30,000-worth of value which can be offered as security on which the bank will take a second mortgage.

You might find that your bank are less generous than you expect in the amount they are prepared to lend. Since property values are almost certainly going to increase, the margin between market value and outstanding mortgage is going to get bigger, and therefore you would logically expect the bank to be prepared to lend up to £30,000 in the example above. You would be disappointed. You might find the bank prepared to lend no more than £15,000 – half the apparent security value.

The thinking is that if the bank is forced to sell the house, the circumstances will result in a lesser price being obtained than in a normal sale. Also, there will be costs involved, such as solicitors, selling agents etc, all of which will eat into the amount received. Personally, I believe banks are a little over-cautious in this respect, and my advice would be to shop around because you might find that different banks (even different branches of the same bank) have different approaches to this.

In the past, the first mortgage on the house would almost always be held by a building society, but now that banks are active in the mortgage market, there is a good chance that you got your mortgage from your bank. In that case, the bank will already hold your house as security, but the same principles will apply in respect of the security value for any further borrowing, that is, the difference between market value and mortgage outstanding.

If your house is to be taken as security, the bank will probably want a professional valuation which will be undertaken at your expense. Indeed, all expenses involved in taking the security, no matter which type, will be passed on to you.

Will the bank sell the security?

The simple answer is yes, if there is no other way of recovering the money they have lent to you. But it really would be a last resort. The bank will be as flexible as they can, and will give you every chance to repay before disposing of your security. If it is possible to repay but it looks as though it is going to take longer than originally anticipated, then the bank will prefer to give you the extra time rather than sell, provided the extra time is reasonable.

When you originally deposited the security with the bank, you will have signed the bank's standard security forms which give the bank the right to dispose of the security. Therefore, you cannot prevent them from doing this, but the bank will of course credit your account with any surplus money obtained from the sale.

Shares can be sold and life policies surrendered very quickly and inexpensively. The sale of a house, however, can take a very long time, and is expensive. The costs will be deducted by the solicitor who is handling the documentation, and the remaining proceeds will be sent to the bank. You receive any surplus, and therefore it is you who are ultimately paying the costs.

There is much more moral stigma attached to selling a customer's house than there is to selling shares or surrendering life policies, and for this reason banks prefer to take shares or life policies rather than residential property. But as stated earlier, a house is very often the only thing of sufficient value that the customer possesses, and do not think that because of the stigma, your bank will not sell – they will, if necessary.

Business assets as security

If your business owns assets which are attractive to the bank as security, these will be taken in preference to your personal assets. Selling the factory is much more palatable to the bank than selling the family home. Having said that, the only asset in which the bank will be interested is freehold or long leasehold property.

However, if your business is a limited company the banks are often interested in taking a special type of security (applicable *only* to limited companies) called a debenture. This document gives *all* the assets of the company to the bank as security – premises, plant, machinery, debtors, stock – the lot! – everything which the company owns.

Giving the bank a debenture does not in any way restrict the company's activities. It gives the bank a *fixed* charge over certain assets such as premises, which means that the premises cannot be sold without the bank's agreement – but that is just like an ordinary mortgage.

Over other assets such as vehicles and stock, the debenture gives the bank a *floating* charge, which allows the company complete freedom to use those assets without having to get the bank's agreement. The company could sell some of its vehicles and use the proceeds as it thinks fit. The stocks can be sold (or used if they are raw materials) whenever the company wishes to do so. It has to be this way, because it would be impossible for the company to trade if the bank's permission were needed every time an item of stock were to be sold or used.

The floating charge was so named to describe its effect. Think of it as an eagle in the sky. It hovers above certain assets, which you are free to use until such time as the company runs into difficulties, and is unable to repay its borrowing to the bank. Then the charge swoops down on to those assets, and fixes them so that they can no longer be used.

Special types of security

As the heading suggests there are some securities which are only applicable in special circumstances, and I will mention them only very briefly.

(a) When lending to importers, the bank will often be prepared to regard the goods being imported as security. The goods will be stored in the name of the bank in a warehouse until such time as they are sold (finished goods) or taken into the factory (raw materials).

(b) When lending to farmers, the bank might take an agricultural charge, which is a little like a debenture in effect. All the assets of the farm are charged to the bank – tractors, machinery, livestock, growing crops, etc.

(c) When the bank are providing finance for a business to perform a specific contract, the bank might accept the right to the proceeds of the contract as security. In other words, the contract monies are assigned to the bank, which means that the contractor will send the proceeds direct to the bank, not to the customer.

Summary

In only a very small percentage of cases do banks find themselves in a position where they have to sell security in order to recover money lent. This is because they are very careful when assessing the risk involved when lending to a particular business.

You can be confident that when a bank lend to your business and ask for security, they are satisfied that in the present circumstances, your business is capable of repaying. The request for security does not mean they have doubts, and it is only if subsequent, unforeseen events make repayment impossible that the security will be sold.

Let us now look at the security position of our three businesses.

Green Light Electrical Company Ltd

This company has an overdraft limit of £175,000, and the bank are being asked to increase it to £200,000. The bank hold a debenture, and the freehold land and buildings were valued recently at £75,000. As mentioned earlier, a debenture gives the bank a charge over all the company's assets, which are valued in the latest balance sheet at:

	£
Freehold land and buildings	60,000
Plant and equipment	28,000
Motor vehicles	42,000
Stock	460,000
Debtors	270,000
	860,000

On the face of it, the bank have substantial security cover for lending of £200,000. You will recall that for this company, we have later management figures for stock and debtors which show stock at the same figure of £460,000 and debtors at £235,000 – therefore, little change.

However, you will also recall that this company is making losses, and therefore the bank will look very critically at the security values of each asset. The bank will consider what their position would be if the company went into liquidation, which looks a distinct possibility. In these situations, the bank will drastically reduce balance sheet valuations in order to look at the worst possible position:

(a) *Land and buildings* – recently valued at £75,000 but in a *forced* sale would fetch maybe £60,000. Therefore balance sheet valuation will be left unchanged.

(b) *Plant and equipment* – what is it? – what condition is it in? –

does it have a resale value? The bank will probably disregard it – value nil.

(c) *Vehicles* – how old are they? – what condition are they in? The bank will probably reduce balance sheet valuation by half – value £20,000 approx.

(d) *Stock* – is it all saleable? Sometimes suppliers of stock have a prior claim on it until it has been paid for (applies especially to imported goods) – is stock subject to prior claims? The bank will probably reduce balance sheet valuation by 25 per cent to 50 per cent – value (say) £250,000.

(e) *Debtors* – are they all good for payment? – any potential bad debts? The bank will inspect an age list of debtors and, depending on what they see, value debtors at around 80 per cent of balance sheet valuation – value £220,000 approx.

The new security values, on a 'break-down' basis compared with balance sheet valuations, will be as follows:

	Balance Sheet	Breakdown
	£	£
Freehold land and buildings	60,000	60,000
Plant and equipment	28,000	Nil
Motor vehicles	42,000	20,000
Stock	460,000	250,000
Debtors	270,000	220,000
	860,000	550,000

Incidentally, if any fixed assets have been bought on hire purchase, the amount outstanding to the HP company would also be deducted from the value of those assets. This is because the HP company would have a prior claim on those assets.

For lending of £200,000, the bank is still covered more than 2½ times, and if the company was profitable the bank would be happy with that situation. But the company is making losses which appear to be increasing, and against that background the bank would start to get a little 'edgy' with their position.

This approach might look unnecessarily pessimistic to you, but the bank will always apply 'knock-down' valuations when their lending looks in danger. Having done so, the bank might think the position is so critical that they appoint a receiver to look after their interests. The power to do this is contained in the debenture.

Some bankers might even apply 'knock-down' values to healthy, thriving companies at the time of lending, just to see what their worst position might be, but personally I feel this is being over-cautious.

Fire Tyres Ltd
This company has an overdraft limit of £25,000 which is secured by a debenture. The freehold property is worth £40,000. The company wants to borrow a further £55,000 in order to buy a garage which is being sold for £60,000, which is made up of £50,000 for the freehold site, and £10,000 for plant and equipment. They offer the new site as additional security.

Therefore total borrowing by this company will be £80,000 against the security of the existing debenture and the new freehold site. Balance sheet valuation of the debenture is:

	£
Land and buildings	6,900
Machinery and plant	24,400
Goodwill	2,700
Cash	17,300
Debtors	20,700
Stock	39,000
	111,000

Many of these assets are the same as discussed in Green Light's case, and the same comments will apply. Goodwill would be disregarded because you have to remember that the bank are looking at the situation as if the company has gone into liquidation, and then of course goodwill would be worthless. It should be written out of the accounts.

Cash would also be disregarded because this was the bank balance at balance sheet date. In any case, most of it must now have disappeared because the company is asking the bank to lend £55,000, out of a purchase price of £60,000.

Land and buildings are now worth £40,000 which, applying the pessimistic approach, would fetch on a forced sale (say) £30,000. New security valuations (compared to balance sheet valuations) will therefore be:

	Balance Sheet	Breakdown
	£	£
Land and buildings	6,900	30,000
Machinery and plant	24,400	Nil
Goodwill	2,700	Nil
Cash	17,300	Nil
Debtors	20,700	16,000
Stock	39,000	20,000
	111,000	66,000

For the existing lending of £25,000, the security cover is good. For the new lending (total £80,000) the bank is also offered another freehold property worth £50,000. The bank would have this professionally valued, and if £50,000 is realistic, they would be lending £80,000 against security worth £116,000 (the new plant and equipment would be disregarded).

The bank would regard lending £80,000 against security worth £116,000 (of which only £80,000 is property) as being very generous. They would not be happy with their security margin. But this is where the pessimistic, knock-down approach to security values is, in my opinion, wrong. This company shows no sign of going into liquidation. Completely the reverse: it is strong and profitable.

By the time this company goes into liquidation, if it ever does, the loan to buy the garage will have been reduced and the property values will have increased, which will provide a bigger security margin automatically. It is true that commercial property is more vulnerable to falls in value than residential property, but there is a danger that if bankers become too cautious, they see potential problems everywhere, and never lend a penny!

If you were the directors of Fire Tyres Ltd, I think you could expect your bank to be a little more positive in their approach. Lending £80,000 to a profitable company against properties with balance sheet values of £90,000 and other assets in the background should warrant a favourable response from the bank.

AB Equipment

The bank are asked to lend £100,000 so that the business can buy the premises it presently rents. Of this, £50,000 will be repaid in four months, and the remaining £50,000 over ten years. The purchase price of the premises is £120,000 and the business is going to spend £10,000 on renovations. The partners have contributed the extra £30,000. The business has no borrowing and the bank have no security.

The obvious security is the property being purchased. It is worth £120,000 now, and more when the renovations have been completed. When the part sale has been completed, the bank will be owed £50,000. But what will the remaining premises be worth? It depends on how large a proportion was sold. The selling price was £50,000 and therefore (presumably) the premises remaining would be worth at least £70,000 (remember they cost £120,000) plus any value that the renovations have added.

The security value would appear to be at least £70,000 against lending of £50,000. As the security is property, this would be just about acceptable to the bank on the basis that the loan would reduce, and the property value would increase, to provide a comfortable margin in due course.

The bank might think about taking the houses of the partners as additional security. However, as the partners have recently increased their mortgages, it could be that the houses have little security value for the bank. A debenture is out of the question, as this business is a partnership, and debentures apply only to limited companies.

Summary

Banks take security as a second line of defence. The most important feature is the business's ability to repay any money lent, and a bank will not lend if repayment prospects are poor, no matter how much security is available.

A margin will be required between the value of the security and the amount lent, to allow for fluctuations in the value of the security. The bank will invariably take a much more conservative view of security values than the customer will.

Remember, the bank will sell if necessary – no matter how harsh the decision might seem to be.

17. Personal Influences

For a banker, lending to a business is not a lot different from giving personal loans, in that even if the bank are lending to a public company, they are still lending essentially to people. It is people with whom the bank manager conducts the interview, it is people who run the business.

Therefore, as well as looking at the numbers, the ratios, the security, and all the other technical sophistications, there is this basic but equally important element, 'Who are we lending to? What do we know about them? Can we rely on them?'.

Character

The personal integrity of businessmen is so important. A bank is not likely to lend to a business unless they feel they can trust the people who run the business.

When faced with a marginal lending proposition which the banker is agonising over and wondering which way to jump, very often the deciding factor will be, 'Will these people let us down?'. Of course, lending can go wrong for a number of reasons but many of them are outside the control of the businessman, eg the price of oil. Banks are aware that nobody can predict the future with absolute accuracy, but they will want to feel confident that borrowers will not leave any stone unturned in their attempts to honour their debts to the bank.

The main factor in judging character is time. The longer the bank have known you, the better they will know you, and for a banker there is no substitute for the confidence in a customer's integrity and honesty that a long association can bring. People change banks much more readily than they did 10 or 20 years ago, which is the product of increased competition between the banks. But I would advise anyone to think long and hard before taking such a step, and having to start from scratch with another bank. You would be throwing away a very valuable asset.

What would it take to make you change banks? The manager being tougher than expected? A refusal to lend? A change of manager at your branch? Think about it, because these are the things which will be going through the mind of the manager of the new bank you have chosen: 'Why is this person coming to my bank?'

You can see that you would have a hill to climb. You have got to establish yourself all over again, and you are going to be viewed with some suspicion. A change of manager at your old bank can sometimes bring a clash of personalities, sufficient to make a customer look elsewhere, but it is rare that such a situation is serious enough for the customer to do that. Bankers know this. Bankers always suspect that when a new business comes their way 'off the street', it is because their present bankers have turned them down. Bankers know that bankers do not turn down good business.

However, I have pointed out on a number of occasions already that not all bankers approach things in exactly the same way. They all receive more or less the same training, but they are people, and some will adopt a more positive attitude than others. If you have had what you consider to be a viable proposition turned down by one of life's pessimists, then you have no option but to try elsewhere. If your opinion of the proposition is correct, then there is no reason why you should not be successful with another bank.

Connection

Leading on from the last point, you would be much better off if, instead of going direct to another bank, you had a word with your accountant. The idea is that, assuming your accountant shares your view that the lending proposition is viable, you can be introduced to your accountant's bank.

Up to the early 1970s, banking was a very sedate business. Bank managers were not expected to go looking for business. Since then, however, banking has become very competitive, and a manager's future prospects depend very much on the amount of new business that he or she can generate for the bank. Consequently, a new breed of bank manager has evolved – one who is marketing-orientated, keen to do business. However, the lending must not be reckless. There is no point in doing masses of new business which all turns out to be bad.

The major source of new business for bankers is the other professional people in town – accountants, solicitors, insurance brokers, estate agents. If they have clients in need of finance, they can help those clients to obtain that finance by introducing them to a banker. For this reason, bankers tend to woo local members of these professions, and will always try to oblige by lending to someone who has been introduced in this way.

Now don't get carried away! Just because your accountant has introduced you, it does not mean that you are automatically going to get what you want. The bank will still go through the normal procedures, but the fact is that the proposition will be viewed more positively than if you had gone in unannounced.

Capability

The bank's view of a person's business acumen is going to play an important part. Now you might think that a business's results speak for themselves – if the business is profitable, the businessman is capable; if losses are being made, the businessman is incapable. I feel certain that as business people you would not subscribe to that argument, and you would be right, because it is not true.

Some people are successful in business because of an initial slice of luck. They happened to be in the right place at the right time, to take advantage of a certain situation. In some cases, the business succeeds in spite of them, not because of them. The ones who have ability build on to their good fortune and develop a business which lasts. Those without ability disappear when their luck runs out.

It is the other side of the scenario which is of more interest. What happens when a business runs into a bad patch, as all businesses do at some time? This is when the continued support of the bank is so important, because it is that which determines whether the business comes through the bad patch, or goes to the wall. Much then depends on the opinion the bank have formed of the people who are running the business. If the bank have confidence in their ability to pull the business through, then the bank will stick with them. Without that confidence, the bank will withdraw their support.

Remember, however, that confidence in people's capabilities does have limits. If recovery of the bank's money is in critical danger, then the bank will have no option but to take action to protect their lending.

Past record

When trying to decide whether to lend, the bank will consider how you have conducted your accounts in the past, both personal and business. This is strongly linked to 'character' in that a person's integrity is the major factor in how that person's affairs are handled.

If you approach your bank to lend to your business, the bank are not going to be too keen to lend if they have had trouble in the past in trying to control your account. For example, if you have been in the habit of going overdrawn without first getting the bank's permission, the bank are going to start suspecting your trustworthiness. Nobody has an automatic right to go overdrawn, and apart from the lack of courtesy on your part, you run the risk of the bank 'bouncing' your cheques. If that happened to a cheque drawn in favour of a supplier, it could cause your business serious damage.

If you have always been straight and honest with your bank, always consulted them when you needed financial assistance, as opposed to 'helping yourself' to an overdraft, you will find that the bank will always try to help you. If you have had problems with the bank, maybe had cheques 'bounced', you are not damned for life, but you are going to have to go through a period of restoring the bank's faith in you. Remember that changing banks is not really the answer in this situation, for reasons already stated.

If you do find yourself in the position of having to approach another bank, that bank will not have the benefit of a past record to consult. Therefore they will ask to see your bank statements for at least the previous 12 months, to try to assess from the conduct of your account how much faith they can place in you.

A very comforting thing for a banker when looking at a lending proposition is to look back and see that you have borrowed previously, and have repaid the loan in accordance with the agreement. Unless the new request is for a much higher amount, there is no reason for the bank to doubt you will honour the new agreement also.

Impressions

In any relationship, people form impressions of others. You want your bank's impression of you to be favourable, and there are a few ways in which you can help yourself.

In this book I have tried to show you how the bank will look at your accounts and at any request to borrow money. You should now be in a better position to anticipate the points which the bank is likely to raise, which should give you the opportunity to have the answers ready. That will impress.

Arrange to see your bank well in advance, if this is possible. About a week before you are due to meet, send your bank copies of your latest accounts together with details of your proposition and any supporting documentation, eg cash flow forecasts, profit projections. There is nothing more frustrating for a bank manager than to have piles of paper thrust across the desk which the manager is supposed to consult while conducting the interview at the same time.

By sending on all this information in advance, you are allowing the banker to become fully conversant with what it is you want, and you are providing him or her with all the background detail which will be needed to reach a decision. You will then find that the interview takes the form of the banker merely trying to clear up areas which are a little doubtful, and hopefully you will have the answers. This would save a great deal of time for both of you, and would be a very professional way of negotiating an overdraft or loan. That would certainly impress.

There is another benefit of doing it this way. Through the process of writing it down, you will be amazed at how much more clearly focused your thoughts become on what it is that you want from the bank. If you just go into an interview with ideas in your head, you can appear very vague indeed, and create completely the wrong impression.

Do not try too hard to impress in other ways. Be yourself. Any hint of 'flashiness' or superficiality is going to ruin your chances. This is especially true if it is your first meeting with a new banker. In point of fact, the preparations described already are going to create a very good first impression on a new banker. Be on time and be presentable. Do not exaggerate.

Remember one thing. A banker's working life consists of meeting and dealing with people. Occasionally they get it wrong, but usually they can assess a person very quickly. They are also slightly cynical. In a lending situation, the customer is wanting something, and is therefore keen to create the right impression of professionalism, honesty and integrity. The cynical side of the banker cannot help but look for flaws in the 'face' you are presenting, looking for you giving yourself away with something you say or do. Obviously, if you are presenting the real you, you have no problem.

What view would the bank take of the three businesses we have been discussing?

Green Light Electrical Company Ltd

This is a long-established company that has hit a bad patch. In the latest year, the company made its first ever loss, but the bank have had a long association with the company (20 years) and therefore will do everything possible to help the company through this period.

However, the overdraft is increasing, and so are the losses. In the management accounts it would appear that a loss in the region of £50,000 has been made in the last nine months. The bank are reasonably well secured, but if losses continue, the bank's security will diminish as the assets diminish.

The bank are in that tricky situation of wanting to help 'old friends' but needing to protect their own position. So much relies on the directors' ability to turn the company round quickly, and the bank's confidence in that ability. The bank will not wait long before appointing a receiver.

Fire Tyres Ltd

The bank's association with this company was formed seven years ago, and the business seems to be very well run. The directors want to borrow an extra £55,000 to expand their interests, and the bank would be highly satisfied with their capability.

AB Equipment

This business has been with the bank for 12 years. They operate in a specialised market and want to borrow to buy their premises.

The partnership has no borrowing at the moment, which means that if they have borrowed in the past, it has been repaid. In other words, their past record looks good. The bank would want very much to help the partners with this proposition because they have had a long association with the bank. However, the business's profitability is not sufficient to service the borrowing and therefore, despite the strong personal influences, the bank will have to refuse.

18. Summary

We will now briefly draw together for each company the various aspects of the lending proposition. Before you read on, you might like to look back at the summary of the audited accounts for each business in Chapter 10.

Green Light Electrical Company Ltd

Purpose and amount

(a) Increase existing overdraft limit from £175,000 to £200,000 for working capital purposes due to losses being made.
(b) This compares to net worth of £250,000 or £220,000 depending on whether directors' loans are included. Either way, £200,000 is very generous.
(c) Hidden reserve of £15,000, but net worth will have reduced due to further losses of around £50,000 in last nine months.
(d) Net worth estimated at 220 + 15 − 50 = £185,000. Overdraft request more than net worth. Cash flow forecast required.

Repayment and term

(a) Overdraft – maximum 12 months.
(b) Cost of borrowing is the interest. Company made loss in latest year.
(c) Can future profits cover interest? Projection required (see pages 91–3).

Security

(a) Debenture worth in latest balance sheet £860,000.
(b) Break-up value probably £550,000.
(c) Reasonable cover, but assets will be depleted if losses continue.

Background

Had account 20 years. Latest year was their first loss.

Summary

(a) Position getting critical. Quick action required to stem losses. Can directors do it?
(b) Bank will probably increase overdraft to £200,000 for three months only.
(c) Monthly management figures will have to be produced (not quarterly).
(d) Bank will monitor position very closely and if there is no sign of improvement in three months' time, they will probably appoint a receiver.

Fire Tyres Ltd

Purpose and amount

(a) £55,000 to buy garage, in addition to existing overdraft of £25,000.
(b) Total borrowing £80,000, net worth £81,400.
(c) To lend £80,000 is very generous. Will any working capital be required for running garage?
(d) Valuation of garage site required.
(e) Will the directors be able to run two businesses?
(f) Does the Memorandum of Association allow the purchase of a garage?

Repayment and term

(a) Loan of £55,000 over 10 years.
(b) Cost of new borrowing (say) £10,000 per annum.
(c) Net profit from tyre business in latest year £17,300 plus depreciation of £7400.
(d) Can this be maintained? Projection required (see pages 93–5).
(e) Is new business viable? Audited accounts required.

Security

(a) Debenture worth in latest balance sheet £111,000.
(b) Break-up value £66,000 plus new freehold property worth £50,000 = £116,000.
(c) Lending of £80,000 against security £116,000 is generous.
(d) However, company is profitable and progressive. Position satisfactory.

Background

Good solid company, well run.

Summary

The amount is generous related to net worth and security, but bank would lend.

AB Equipment

Purpose and amount

(a) £50,000 temporary advance to be repaid in four months. £50,000 loan.
(b) Net worth £72,500. Temporarily amount lent will be in excess of net worth, but permanent relationship is acceptable.
(c) Buying premises and renovating. Acceptable purpose.
(d) Estimates of renovation costs to be seen.

Repayment and term

(a) £50,000 over 10 years.
(b) Cost of borrowing £9000 per annum approximately.
(c) Net profit in latest year £3000 plus depreciation £2500 plus the saving in rent £1500 = £7000.
(d) Profit is insufficient. Will future profits be better? Projection required (see pages 95–7).

Security

(a) None held at present.
(b) Premises being bought could be taken as security.
(c) Worth at least £70,000 – just about adequate.

Background

Long association with this business. Purpose is understandable – they wish to own their premises. Bank would want to help.

Summary

Poor profitability and lack of potential will mean a rejection.

Part 3
Other Sources of Finance

19. Introduction

In this short section, I will briefly outline other ways in which you can obtain finance. Although I have referred to them as other sources, you can still get them from your bank. All banks have subsidiary companies which provide hire purchase, leasing, factoring, etc, and while there are independent organisations offering such services, it is much more convenient to use your own bank as the point of contact. I will refer to these forms of finance as alternative trading finance.

In certain situations, you might be able to raise finance under special schemes to assist in either the start-up or expansion of your business. The terms and conditions of such schemes are subject to frequent change, and therefore there is little point in doing much more than letting you know they exist.

20. Alternative Trading Finance

1. Factoring

A factoring company can provide finance and other useful services to a business. It is concerned with a business's debtors, and is therefore relevant to any business which sells on credit terms.

You might have no option but to offer credit, as this might be the only way you can get business. But it does mean that you have to wait for your cash, which you might need to pay bills. It also means that you cannot take advantage of any discounts which your suppliers might be offering. The obvious solution is to borrow from your bank, and pay interest.

You could, however, factor your debtors. You enter into an agreement with a factoring company which will examine your debtor book in detail, and carry out confidential credit checks on your customers. If satisfied, they will then make a cash advance to you of up to 80 per cent of the debtor total. They then collect the debts and pay the balance of 20 per cent to you after collection.

In effect, you are borrowing from the factoring company instead of the bank. You will be charged interest at a similar rate to overdraft rate, although it might work out a little more expensive than overdraft. However, it is a useful source of finance if the bank is being a little strict with you.

The other services offered by a factoring company are: administration of the sales ledger, and credit protection.

Administration of sales ledger

The factoring company will send out your invoices to your customers, collect payment from them, send out statements and reminders (if necessary) and generally chase slow payers. A charge is made for these services, which will be calculated as a percentage of the debtor total.

This service is essential if you are taking a cash advance, but it can also be taken independently if you do not need the cash option. The major benefit is that it releases you from the burden of debt collecting, and leaves you free to concentrate on production and selling. The cost of the service can be set off against the saving in staff costs which will be achieved by not having to employ someone to do the job.

Many businesses are discouraged from using factoring due to the fact that their customers are aware of it. It is the factoring company which collects the amounts owing, and businessmen do not like subjecting their customers to this intermediary, who might not be as tactful with the customers as they themselves would be. They feel that future relationships with customers might be jeopardised by the loss of personal contact.

Credit protection

As mentioned earlier, a factoring company will carry out confidential credit checks on your customers if they are providing a cash advance. This service can be used even if you do not need the cash advance. It can be extremely useful when you are considering doing business with a new customer.

An extension of credit protection is something called non-recourse factoring. This means that the factoring company takes on the risk of your customers not paying, ie the factoring company will stand the loss if the debtors turn out to be bad debts. As far as you are concerned, you can forget all about your debtors; you now have one debtor only, the factoring company itself, and you know they will pay.

Conditions for factoring

A factoring company will be selective in what they are prepared to take on. The following conditions will normally apply:

(a) The debtors must be well spread, ie no single debtor must represent a significant percentage of the total.
(b) There must not be a large number of debts, each of small amounts. This would make administration of the service cumbersome, and therefore very expensive.
(c) Your bad debt record must be acceptable, that is, you must not have a history of several debts going bad on you.
(d) The factoring company will apply to each of your customers a limit on the amount they are allowed to owe you. The figure will be as a result of the credit check, and is likely to be less than you would want to allow.
(e) You must factor all your debts, not just the doubtful ones.

(f) Each factoring company will have its own minimum limit for sales turnover of clients, eg they might not take on the debts of any business with a sales turnover of less than £250,000.

Bank's attitude to factoring
You will recall that in the section on security, we talked about a debenture. This gives the bank a charge on all the assets of the company (remember a debenture can only be given by a limited company).

Debtors represent an asset of the company, and if a company factors its debtors, the bank will have to give the factoring company priority over this asset. The factoring company would not make a cash advance until it had this priority.

The bank's security cover is therefore going to be weakened, as they are losing part of it. For this reason, the bank might insist that the overdraft is either completely repaid or drastically reduced. This should not be a problem for you, because what you are doing is replacing the bank overdraft with funds borrowed from the factoring company.

You should always regard factoring as an alternative to an overdraft, not to medium-term loans.

2. Invoice discounting

This is another service provided by a factoring company, but it is not nearly as comprehensive as the full factoring service. It involves the selling at a discount of individual invoices to the factoring company.

You have sold goods to a customer on three-month credit terms, and you have a pressing need for cash. You could try to arrange an overdraft (or an increase in the overdraft) but you might prefer to convert that invoice into cash. The factoring company would run a credit check on your debtor, and would calculate the discount based on your customer's creditworthiness. The better the rating, the less the discount.

The advantages to you of invoice discounting over full factoring are:

(a) You can select individual invoices to discount, whereas factoring involves all your debts.
(b) You can use invoice discounting as a 'one-off' exercise, whereas factoring is a continuous service.
(c) You collect the debt yourself in three months' time, and pay

over the proceeds to the factoring company, whereas with factoring it is the factoring company which collects. Therefore, with invoice discounting, you maintain the personal contact with your customer.

(d) You are not paying for the administration service, which is an essential part of factoring when you take a cash advance.

3. Hire Purchase

This will not need much explanation. Most people are familiar with HP on a personal basis, as it is the way that many consumer items are bought, eg cars, washing machines, videos, etc.

Commercial hire purchase for the acquisition of vehicles or plant and machinery works in the same way. You will be expected to contribute part of the cost yourself, borrowing the remainder from the HP company. It is an alternative to arranging a loan from the bank, and is not a substitute for an overdraft.

The period or term of the agreement will usually be geared to the expected life span of the asset being bought – usually three to seven years. You will repay by monthly instalments over that period.

With commercial hire purchase, you will find that you can negotiate much more flexible terms than are possible with personal hire purchase. For example, the repayment instalments can be varied, with low amounts in the early years increasing in later years.

Legally you do not own the asset until the last instalment has been made. However, the asset is shown in the balance sheet as soon as you acquire it, and the debt to the HP company is shown as a current liability. The HP company has first claim on the asset if repayments are not kept up or if the business goes bankrupt or into liquidation.

4. Leasing

This is a third method of acquiring assets such as vehicles or plant and machinery. It is an alternative to either a bank loan or commercial hire purchase.

The essential difference of this method concerns ownership. You never own a leased asset (although there are leasing agreements which include an option to purchase). Usually the leasing company retains ownership, and you pay a monthly rental for the use of the asset.

As with HP, the agreement is drawn up for a period which will cover the useful life of the asset. Flexible terms can be arranged, eg rentals can be the same throughout or on an increasing basis. Since you are not buying, no deposit is required although you will probably have to pay (say) a quarter's rental in advance.

Leasing is usually concerned with vehicles. Trucks and vans can be leased as well as cars, although cars are the most commonly leased assets. There are two main types of lease:

(a) Finance lease, where you remain responsible for servicing, maintenance and repairs. The original agreement will usually contain an assessment of what the value of the car should be at the end of the leasing period. If the actual value is less, you have to pay the difference; if it is worth more, you receive the difference. So it is wise to look after it.

(b) Operating lease, which is much more comprehensive. The leasing company is responsible for servicing, maintenance and repairs, and normally for other things such as insurance, break-down charges, and even membership of one of the motoring organisations. Operating leasing, which is also referred to as contract hire, is obviously more expensive than finance leasing.

5. Sale and leaseback

If you own the freehold of your business premises, you can raise finance by selling them to a financial institution and then leasing them from that institution. Insurance companies and pension funds are heavy investors in property, and an agreement could be made with such an institution.

Many businesses find themselves in the strange position of being short of working capital for day-to-day business needs, while at the same time holding a substantial asset in the balance sheet in the form of premises. The cash which is tied up in that asset can be released by entering into a sale and leaseback agreement.

You must make sure that the period of the lease suits your purposes. For example, a short-term lease might cause problems because you might not be able to renew it. However, if you are due to retire in ten years' time, a short-term lease might be ideal.

The disadvantage with sale and leaseback is that you are giving up the only asset in the balance sheet which appreciates in value.

You will be forfeiting future increases in the value of your business, which are brought about by appreciation in the value of freeholds.

For this reason, most businesses prefer to borrow on overdraft from their bank for working capital, and offer their premises as security. But, as we have seen in Part 2, banks sometimes refuse to lend even when there is adequate security available. If you find yourself in that situation, then sale and leaseback might be your only alternative.

21. Special Schemes

During the 1980s there have been several attempts to promote small businesses. The major problem with new businesses was finding suitable finance, because they have no track record to give comfort to a lender. Businesses which wanted to expand found similar problems because lenders were afraid that these businesses might overstretch themselves and run into difficulties.

The government set the mood of assistance for small businesses with the introduction of the Small Firms Loan Guarantee Scheme and the Business Start-up Scheme. With this encouragement, banks started putting together packages specially designed to assist with start-up or expansion.

Small Firms Loan Guarantee Scheme

The Government introduced the scheme in 1981. This is not a scheme which provides finance, but it does make it easier for you to obtain finance from your bank. The scheme applies to sole traders, partnerships and limited companies.

You may recall that when a bank are looking at a lending proposition, they are usually loath to lend more than the business's net worth. The bank are also likely to want security. If either of these criteria is not met, it is doubtful if a bank will be willing to lend.

The Loan Guarantee Scheme was introduced to persuade banks to look favourably at propositions which did not fully satisfy their normal lending requirements. A business could apply for a Government guarantee in respect of the amount which they wanted to borrow.

The application had to be processed through a bank, which had to add their recommendation. Therefore the bank had to be satisfied that the prospects of repayment were good, and that the reason they were not prepared to lend was because of a weakness in one of the other previously mentioned areas.

If satisfied, the Government, through the Department of Trade and Industry, would guarantee 80 per cent of the loan (although this has subsequently been lowered to 70 per cent). For example, a business which wants a loan of £50,000 but which has security worth only £25,000 might be rejected by the bank because of inadequate security. However, a government guarantee of £35,000, together with the business security of £25,000, makes the loan fully secured.

Applications have to be supported by detailed business plans and projections, and a premium has to be paid for the guarantee. There is a maximum amount applied to loans for which guarantees will be provided, and the scheme is not available for certain trades or businesses. The scheme cannot be used to replace existing borrowing.

Details in the previous paragraph have been left deliberately vague because they are constantly liable to change. The best bet is to ask your bank for up-to-date information.

Business Expansion Scheme

This scheme was introduced in the 1983 budget to replace the Business Start-up Scheme. It extends the availability of funds to existing businesses, whereas the original scheme was for new ventures only.

It is a method of raising substantial sums of money. Your first point of contact should be your bank, who will call in their merchant bank subsidiary to advise on the matter.

The money which you raise under the BES belongs to individual investors. They get tax relief at their highest rate on money put into BES ventures, but they must hold on to their investment for five years. The maximum investment for an individual or for a married couple is £40,000 – but this could be changed in subsequent budgets.

The merchant bank subsidiary of your bank will suggest the best way of raising the money. It might mean the issue of a prospectus inviting direct investment, or perhaps the use of a BES fund, which is a pool of BES investment money. In the latter case, the fund manager might insist on a seat on your board.

This is a very specialised form of raising capital, and your business will have reached substantial proportions before you can qualify for BES funding. The individual investors will be hoping that your company will progress to the Unlisted Securities Market or even to a full stock market listing. This will make it easier for them to recoup their investment because they will be able to sell their shares. It is not going to be easy for them if your company has not progressed in this way.

Individual bank packages

As stated elsewhere, banks are traditionally short-term lenders. As recently as the mid 1970s, banks were not heavily into providing term loans for the purchase of business premises. The major source of such funds was the insurance companies.

Times have changed dramatically. Nowadays medium- and long-term loans are marketed vigorously by the banks – even personal mortgages.

All the major banks now provide special types of loan designed for either business start-ups or expansion. Such loans would typically include the following features:

(a) Period of loan can be anything between five and 20 years.
(b) Repayment programme can be tailored to individual needs, ie standard level of repayment throughout or different levels at different times.
(c) Capital holidays can be arranged, ie only interest will be paid in the first one or two years; there will be no capital reductions during this time. This is helpful to cash flow in the early stages of the loan.
(d) Interest can be fixed at the same rate throughout the loan, or can be geared to Base Rate and therefore fluctuate as Base Rate changes, eg 3 per cent over Base Rate.

Banking is so competitive now that individual banks are constantly bringing out new packages in an attempt to attract business customers. As you read this, there will be schemes which were not in existence at the time of writing.

The message is to shop around. So long as you have a sound business, you will be able to find a scheme to suit you. Remember, though, that a long association with a bank is a valuable asset to you. Try your own bank first – they will do all they can to meet your requirements.

4. Venture capital

Venture capital is risk capital. This can be provided by an organisation called 3is – Investment in Industry – in which all the banks have an interest.

Each individual bank can also provide venture capital through their merchant bank subsidiary. The funds provided can be a combination of equity (ie shares in your company) and loans. The bank will never want a majority shareholding and will not interfere with the day-to-day running of the company. But they will require regular reports on performance, and often will want a non-executive seat on your board.

The minimum amount provided will vary from bank to bank, but it is unlikely that cases of less than £100,000 would be considered.

22. Summary

The object of Part 3 has been to make you aware of other types of finance and assistance which are available outside the confines of normal bank activities.

While these services are also provided by independent bodies, it is possible to get them through your bank. Banks have extended the range of their services by taking over companies which specialise in these areas. Most of the major banks own subsidiary companies which can provide everything which has been described in these pages.

There are independent financial advisers and there is your accountant, all of whom could point you to the most relevant source for your requirements. However, the banks have spent a great deal in training their managers to be more than just lenders, and they pride themselves these days on having a wide understanding of the needs of modern business.

They make an excellent focal point.

Part 4
Buying a Business

23. Introduction

In this section, we are going to look at a specific lending situation, as opposed to the general approach covered in Part 2.

You might be brand new to business, that is you are reading this book as one of the thousands of people who, each year, venture into business for the first time. For you, I will go through the items which make up the annual accounts.

On the other hand, you might already be in business, and you are wanting to buy another outlet or maybe you intend to diversify into something else. Perhaps you are managing a business, and now you have the opportunity to buy it.

For all of you, the bank will raise certain points when you ask for finance, eg your previous experience, the reason the business is being sold, what assets you are actually buying, how viable the business is. The extent of these questions will depend on the circumstances, and we will examine each in turn.

24. Annual Accounts

You will have to keep daily records of all your business transactions, eg purchase of supplies, payment of electricity bill, receipts for goods sold, etc. This can be done in a simple cashbook obtainable from any stationer's. You might also have to register for VAT. You will need to speak to an accountant – the sooner the better.

At the end of your first year, and every succeeding year, your accountant will produce the annual accounts for your business, which consist of:

(a) Trading account
(b) Profit and loss account
(c) Balance sheet

Trading account

This is constructed as follows:

	£		£
Opening Stock	Nil	Sales	130,000
Purchases	100,000		
	100,000		
Less Closing Stock	10,000		
Cost of Goods Sold	90,000		
Gross Profit	40,000		
	130,000		130,000

Notes.

(a) In the first year, there is no opening stock (unless you buy an existing business). In the second year, your opening stock will be £10,000, ie this year's closing stock, carried forward.

(b) Purchases – the amount of supplies you bought during the year.
(c) Closing stock – the amount of stock you have left at the end of the year.
(d) Cost of goods sold – the cost of the goods you have actually sold, ie the cost of the stock you have used in achieving your sales.
(e) Gross profit – the difference between your sales and your costs.
(f) Sales – the income from sales for the year.

Profit and loss account

This is constructed as follows:

	£		£
Electricity	1,500	Gross Profit	40,000
Gas	1,000		
Telephone	1,200		
Stationery	2,000		
Salaries	15,000		
etc	etc		
Overheads	32,000		
Net Profit	8,000		
	40,000		40,000

Notes.

(a) Gross profit is carried down from the trading account.
(b) The various items of expenditure (known as overheads) are listed down the left-hand side.
(c) Net profit – the profit which is left after the overheads have been deducted from the gross profit. This is the amount which is left for you as proprietor.

Balance sheet

This is a statement of the business's assets and liabilities, as at the close of business on the last day of your business year. Assets are the things which the business *owns*, liabilities are the things which the business *owes*.

The following balance sheet is not intended to relate to any particular type of business, but is just a list of the more common items, eg a retail business would not have work-in-progress.

Liabilities		Assets	
Capital Reserves Profit and Loss	(A)	Premises Plant and Machinery Vehicles Fixtures and Fittings Goodwill	(C)
Creditors Bank Hire Purchase Tax	(B)	Stock Work-in-Progress Debtors Bank	(D)

Note. This list is not exhaustive.

(A) Permanent liabilities

These liabilities can be collectively referred to in a number of ways, eg permanent liabilities, proprietor's stake, capital base. In other parts of the book, I refer to them as net worth.

1. *Capital*

This is the amount of money put into the business by the proprietor(s). For a limited company, it would be share capital; for a partnership or sole trader, it would be referred to just as capital or perhaps shown as capital accounts.

Many people find it difficult to understand why capital should be a liability – it sounds like an asset. You have to think in terms of a liability being money owed by the business – in this case the business owes that money to the proprietor(s).

2. *Reserves*

This item will be seen only with limited company accounts. There are two types of reserves:

(a) Revenue reserves – these are accumulated profits from normal trading. If the company makes a net profit each year, then the revenue reserves should increase each year by the amount of the net profit.

(b) Capital reserves – these can be created in a number of ways, but the range of possibilities is outside the objectives of this book. The two prime examples (as far as the bank will be concerned) are where premises have been revalued and where an asset has been sold at a profit.

In the first case, let us say that the premises were bought five years ago for £50,000. This will show as an asset (premises) of £50,000. If the premises are revalued at £80,000, then a 'profit' of £30,000 has been made. The premises figure would be increased from £50,000 to £80,000, and a new item of £30,000 would appear on the liabilities side, ie capital reserve. In other words, the value of the business has increased by £30,000.

In the second case, let us say that a vehicle shown in the balance sheet at £4000 is sold for £5000. It would be misleading to include this in normal trading profits, and therefore £1000 is shown as a capital reserve.

3. *Profit and loss*

This item will be seen where the business is a partnership or a sole proprietor, and it is often seen in company accounts instead of revenue reserves. It is the accumulated total of past profits left in the business. It increases each year if profits are made, and decreases if losses are made. Very often with partnerships or sole proprietors, the P & L will be part of the capital account shown in the balance sheet, eg:

	£
Capital Account	17,000
Add Profits	21,000
	38,000
Less Drawings	16,000
	22,000

(a) £17,000 is the balance of the capital account brought forward from the previous year.

(b) £21,000 is the net profit made during the year.

(c) £16,000 represents the amount withdrawn by the proprietor for personal uses.
(d) £22,000 is the new capital account balance which will be carried forward into the following year.

(B) Current Liabilities

The definition of current liabilities is debts which are due to be paid within the next 12 months. With limited companies, accountants include in current liabilities any loans made to the company by the directors, although these monies might never be withdrawn.

The total amount of current liabilities is obviously very important to both you and your bank, because they are short-term debts which will have to be paid. Your bank will be interested in how you are going to meet these liabilities, because unless you have sufficient current assets which can be converted to cash very quickly, you will have to borrow.

1. *Creditors*

These are people to whom the business owes money as at balance sheet date. This will include suppliers and any other bills outstanding, such as electricity. Some accountants show separate totals for trade creditors (suppliers) and other creditors, but usually only one figure is shown.

2. *Bank*

If this item appears on the liabilities side of the balance sheet, it represents money owing to the bank. You might have several accounts at the bank, but only the combined balance will be shown.

3. *Hire purchase*

If you buy any of the assets by borrowing from a finance company under a hire purchase agreement, the amount outstanding will be shown in the balance sheet.

4. *Tax*

Businesses pay tax on profits at certain times of the year. At the end of your business year, you will probably have an amount outstanding which is due to be paid to the Inland Revenue in a few months' time. It does not necessarily mean that the amount is overdue.

(C) Fixed assets

From the very name, it can be assumed that these assets will not change in value on a day-to-day basis. They are necessary for the business to perform, but they will waste away over a period of time. You are allowed to show these assets at a lower value each year to reflect this wasting. This is called depreciation.

1. Premises

(a) This might be shown as land and buildings if you own the freehold of the premises. Freehold relates to the title to the premises – a freeholder is the absolute owner. This asset will usually increase in value, ie appreciate as opposed to depreciate.

(b) However, you might only hold a lease over the premises, that is they belong to someone else but you have the right to use them for a period of years. The attitude to the value of the lease will depend upon the term of years.

All leases will be worthless when the period has expired, and therefore short leases (21 years or less) should be depreciated in the balance sheet each year, ie the value should be written down.

A longer-term lease (say 99 years or more) will behave more like leaseholds on domestic property (999 years). In other words, it is common to see them appreciate in value, but maybe not so much as freeholds. But long leases too will depreciate as the term nears expiry.

A short-term lease which has not been depreciated in the balance sheet will make the business look more valuable than it is.

2. Plant and machinery

This is usually the heavy equipment on which goods are manufactured.

3. Vehicles

This can be anything from lorries to delivery vans to directors' cars.

4. Fixtures and fittings

This asset is usually found in the balance sheet of a retailer, and relates to things like display cabinets, refrigeration units etc.

5. *Goodwill*

This is an asset which most people understand but which is difficult to define. It is an intangible asset which tries to put a value on the custom or business which the proprietor has built up.

When a business is being sold, the vendor will want some sort of recompense for his efforts and for the fact that he is giving up to someone else the fruits of his success. Therefore the selling price will be comprised not only of tangible assets such as fixtures and fittings and stock, but also a figure for goodwill. This will be based on either annual sales or profits.

(D) Current assets

These assets will change in value every day. Stock will be sold (or used, if raw materials), cash will be received or a customer debt created.

The relationship between current assets and current liabilities is vital to a business. When an asset is close to being converted into cash it is said to be liquid, eg stocks of finished goods are more liquid than stocks of raw materials. If finished goods are always sold on credit, then debtors will be more liquid than finished goods.

A business must have sufficient current assets to satisfy current liabilities, when they are due for payment. Otherwise fixed assets would have to be sold (this would be disastrous) or money would have to be borrowed.

1. *Stock*

A retail or wholesale business will usually have only one type of stock – finished goods ready for sale.

A manufacturer will have stocks of raw materials, stocks of partly finished goods and stocks of finished goods.

Each business has to ascertain by experience what the correct stock levels are for that particular business. Too little can affect sales, ie poor range of goods; too much ties up cash for long periods, which can be expensive if you have borrowed to buy stock.

2. *Work-in-progress*

This asset is usually seen in building and construction businesses. All incomplete projects have to be given a value as a balance sheet date.

3. *Debtors*

It is much better to sell for cash than it is to sell on credit.

There are two main advantages:

(a) You have the cash to pay your bills. If you sold on credit, you might have to borrow.

(b) You will not have the inconvenience of collecting the debts or the problem of bad debts, ie your customer not paying.

Unfortunately, you might have no choice but to sell on credit. It might be the only way you can get business. If this is the case, then all money owing to you from customers as at balance sheet date will be shown as debtors.

4. *Bank*

If this item appears on the assets side of the balance sheet, it means that the business has money in the bank.

Summary

Let me remind you that your annual accounts will be prepared by a qualified accountant. You have to submit audited accounts (signed by an accountant) to the Inland Revenue for tax purposes.

All that you need to do is to make sure that you record all items of income and expenditure, and that you keep all receipts for money spent.

Just a final point about the accounts of a manufacturing business. Your accountant might produce a manufacturing account in addition to the others already discussed. It will be constructed like the trading account.

The left-hand side of the manufacturing account will list all the costs of manufacture, eg raw materials, wages, factory rent, etc. The right-hand side will be a balancing item labelled 'Cost of manufacture of finished goods, carried down to trading account'. The balancing item will be transferred to the left-hand side of the trading account, and will replace the items for opening stock and purchases shown in our trading account earlier. In other words, the business is manufacturing its finished goods, rather than purchasing them from another supplier.

25. Previous Experience

To run a business successfully, you need the skills of the trade and also management skills. It is one thing to know everything about car engines, and quite another to run a car repair shop. To do the latter you need to be able to deal with customers, representatives and your banker, and to be able to cost jobs properly in order to make a profit. You will also have to deal with the people who work for you, be a salesman, a stock controller, a bookkeeper, and so on.

Experience of trade or business

Bankers are well aware that some businesses require a higher level of personal skill than others. The various trades – electrician, plumber, builder, etc – can only be undertaken by people who have had the necessary training or apprenticeship. Any sort of manufacturing activity is going to require specialist knowledge.

Without wishing to sound derogatory to the retail trade, I would say that to run any sort of retail business (buying and selling) does not require the same level of speciality. Obviously, there are things which have to be learned (eg the various cuts of meat if you are a butcher) but they are things which can be picked up much more quickly than can the skills of the manufacturer.

Management experience

When you approach the bank for finance, you are going to be in a much stronger position if you can show that you have had previous experience of actually running a business. Any type of business will do for this purpose, but so much the better if it has been gained in the type which you are wanting to buy.

The extent of previous experience will vary. It might be that you have been in charge whenever the boss has been away, eg holidays or sickness. On the other hand, you might have been, for many years, the manager of the business which you now want to buy. For example, the manager of a public house or a newsagent's shop might be given the chance to buy. In this situation, you are in the strongest position of all. You know the business inside out – margins, stock levels etc.

For small businesses, banks expect the owner to be closely involved on a day-to-day basis. For example, I have over 20 years' experience in banking and finance, but a bank would not feel comfortable if I wanted to borrow to buy a car repair shop, and I intended to employ someone to run it for me.

As businesses grow, other outlets or branches might be opened. As this happens, the owner is going to get further and further removed from daily operational problems. This is unavoidable, but it is a different matter from buying your first shop and leaving it to someone else to make it successful.

Franchising

A good way to start out in business is to enter into a franchised operation. This combines the attraction of being self-employed with the benefit of not being completely on your own. It is estimated that as many as 90 per cent of new franchises succeed. You have an organisation in the background who can give guidance and support.

The High Streets are full of franchised businesses, from fast food restaurants, such as pizza houses, to dry cleaning shops. They are run by people like you, who pay a sum of money to buy such things as fixtures and fittings, stock etc.

It is your business but you have the advantage of the franchisor's name, the benefit of their national advertising, probably some training, guidance on bookkeeping and assessing stock levels, etc. You will also reap the benefit of the company's ability to buy stock at favourable prices due to the size of their bulk-buying activities. In return, you will have to pay them an agreed percentage of your profits or sales.

Many people find this the safest and most comforting way to set up in business, and banks will look more favourably at a proposition which has a well-run reputable organisation behind it. Many banks now provide special lending schemes geared to franchised operations.

The down side for you is that you never really feel that you are the boss. Although you have complete freedom in day-to-day management, there is always the knowledge that, somewhere in the background, there is someone to whom you are accountable – and who takes some of your hard-earned income.

Summary

Every year, many people take the plunge and set up on their own, and a high percentage of them fail. Banks adopt a very cautious approach when considering lending propositions of this nature because the risks are so high.

You will have to present a very strong case, and unless you can show some measure of previous experience, you are unlikely to get a bank to support you.

26. Reason for Selling

There are any number of reasons why the proprietor of a business might want to sell, and the bank's fear will be that the business is not profitable. It is easy enough to find out merely by examining the audited accounts of the business, but we will say more about that in Chapter 28, Viability of Business.

Retirement

A business might come on the market due to the retirement of the present owner. The bank would want to know what has been happening to the business in the last couple of years or so, because many people retire unofficially two years before they do so officially.

It would not be uncommon to find a falling off in sales in recent years, as the proprietor loses interest and 'winds down' as retirement approaches. The point is, can those lost sales be recovered?

Ill health

Similar considerations will apply here. The proprietor might have been physically incapable of devoting time to the business, resulting in lost sales turnover.

Death

If the proprietor has died, the most important question is, how long ago did he die? What has happened to the business in the meantime? Has it ceased to do business or has someone else been running it? If so, who? Have sales been lost?

Lack of profits

This is a valid reason for a proprietor to sell a business, but obviously it is not going to be easy to sell.

If you are asking your bank to finance the purchase of such a business, you have got to be able to provide very good reasons why you think you can do better than the previous owner, eg ill health of the previous owner.

The bank will want detailed projections of what you think you can achieve, but let us leave this for further discussion in Chapter 28, Viability of Business.

27. Composition of Purchase Price

The bank will want to see a break-down of the purchase price into the component parts: premises, fixtures and fittings, stock, etc. In other words, what are you getting for your money? Are you getting value for money?

Each case will be different but the price will be made up of a combination of the following:

(a) Premises

Are they freehold or leasehold? If the latter, is the lease long- or short-term?

Freeholds and long leaseholds will appreciate in value, whereas short leases should be depreciated in the balance sheet every year, down to nil on expiry of the term.

You will need to look very carefully at the valuation placed on a short-term lease. There is a tendency for them to be overvalued by the seller, and you would be advised to obtain a professional valuation by an estate agent. Certainly the bank will want to see a valuation before agreeing to lend.

(b) Fixtures and fittings

What condition are these in? Will they need replacing in the near future? The bank will want you to answer these questions because they know that you will have to approach them for extra finance when the time comes. The bank will not want to assist you with the purchase price only to find you returning six months later for more money. They will want to see the whole picture at the outset.

(c) Plant and machinery

These assets will be seen primarily in a manufacturing business, and the same points will apply as mentioned in respect of fixtures and fittings.

(d) Vehicles

What are they? Are they an integral part of the business, eg lorries in a haulage business? If so, they will be part of the purchase price. What condition are they in? Is the price reasonable? Will replacements or additional vehicles be required?

With many small businesses, the proprietor's car is often shown as a business asset. This will not be part of the purchase price as the proprietor will obviously keep the car. If there was hire purchase outstanding on the car, then this would be shown in the balance sheet as a current liability. Obviously, the proprietor would retain the HP liability as well as the car.

(e) Stock

What is the stock – raw materials, partly finished goods, or finished goods? The big question mark relates to the quality of the stock. If raw materials, are they good and usable? If finished goods, are they all readily saleable or are some obsolete? The fashion industry is vulnerable to having stocks of unsaleable goods as fashions change.

It will be useful to compare stock turnover ratios for the past three years or so. If the rate of turnover is slowing down (ie it is taking longer for stock to turn over) this could be an indication of obsolete stock – see Part 1, p. 42.

(f) Debtors

If goods are sold on credit, it is likely that you will be purchasing debtors. Are they all good? Are there any debts which are bad or doubtful?

You will need an age list of debtors to check out this point.

(g) Goodwill

Part of the purchase price will be goodwill. This is based on either profits or annual sales, and you will need to be careful that you are not paying more than is justified.

Vendors are often greedy in the value they place on goodwill, and it is no easy matter for you to assess whether it is fair or not. There are no strict guidelines and the best bet is for you to consult your accountant on this matter.

28. Viability of Business

Your enthusiasm to buy a particular business can cause you to overlook the fact that it is not very profitable. To be successful in business it is necessary to be positive and optimistic, but you must not rush into something without examining it fully.

Audited accounts

It is essential that you study the accounts of the business for at least the last three years. The business must make sufficient profits to provide you with a satisfactory standard of living, both now and in the future. The bank will also want to see that the profits will cover the interest on the money you borrow from them, and repay the capital if you borrow by way of a loan.

The bank will look particularly closely at:

(a) The gross profit margins to see if there is any significant change over the years.
(b) The size and control of overheads.
(c) The amount of net profit – the source of the bank's repayment.
(d) The growth in sales to see what potential the business has.
(e) Any other significant items, eg increasing stock levels, potential bad debts etc.

Projections

In addition to looking at what has happened in the past, the bank will want you to provide projections of what you think you can achieve in the coming 12 months.

You will need to project sales, gross profit, overheads and net profit, and you might need the help of your accountant. The projection must be realistic, based on what has been achieved in the past. For example, if sales have been growing by around 10 per cent per annum, then the bank are not going to believe a projection showing 25 per cent growth next year.

Banks are often faced by people who are convinced that they

can achieve better results than the previous owner. The bank are going to be sceptical unless there are very good reasons to support your view, eg protracted illness of previous owner. That scepticism is going to be even greater if this is your first business venture, and you cannot therefore point to any previous experience to back up your claims.

Let us look at an example which we have mentioned previously. The manager of a branch of a national chain of newsagent's shops has the chance to buy his outlet. He approaches his bank for finance and produces a projection which shows much better margins than have ever been achieved before. His reasons are that he was restricted by the national company and he can now introduce some of his own ideas. He is also prepared to work much harder now that the profits are going to be his. Reasonable argument? What will the bank make of it?

There are two things which the bank will be very wary of:

(a) The national company would have the benefit of bulk buying, which would improve gross margins. The customer is not going to have that advantage when he goes it alone, and this must reduce his gross margins. Projections showing improvements must be suspect.
(b) The reason for sale would have to be investigated. Perhaps the national company is rationalising its organisation by selling off some of its outlets. It would not be likely to sell the more profitable ones or the ones with great potential.

New units

We have tended so far to talk about situations where an existing business is being bought. Very often, however, a customer is buying a brand new unit in a new complex – an empty shell.

This is the toughest prospect of all. You have no track record to go on. You have to start from scratch; to create business; to find customers.

The bank will be asking a number of questions, which you should have asked yourself already. Is there a need for that particular business in that location? How much competition is there? What levels of business do you expect? What are your projections? What do you base them on?

You will have to be very persuasive if you are to get the bank to support a venture like this. You will have to provide the major part of the finance yourself, and the bank will have to be well secured for any money they lend.

29. Summary

You will need to be very well prepared when you see the bank manager. The banks are well aware of the high failure rate of new businesses.

Essentially, the bank are providing risk capital and will therefore expect you to be prepared to take a bigger risk than they are. In other words, you will have to be putting in more of your own money than you are asking the bank to contribute. While it is impossible to be dogmatic, a rough rule of thumb would be two-thirds from you, and one-third from the bank. Even then, the bank would need adequate security cover.

Before you approach the bank for finance, it would be better to talk to an accountant who will help you to prepare figures for the interview. If you are new to business you might also contact your local Small Firms Service, who could put you on the right track. You can find them in your telephone directory or dial 100 and ask for Freefone Enterprise. You might also be able to get a grant from your local council.

If you are unemployed and have £1000 of your own money to put into a business venture, you can apply for assistance under the Government's Enterprise Allowance Scheme. If successful, you will be paid £40 per week for a year, which is an attempt by the Government to get people through that tricky first year. However, in the first three years of the scheme, only just over 50 per cent of such businesses had survived. You can find out more about the scheme from your local Jobcentre or Manpower Services Commission.

If you started reading this book at Part 4, you can learn much more about the bank's approach to balance sheets and lending propositions in Parts 1 and 2. It might pay you to read those before asking the bank for money.

Further Reading from Kogan Page

Be Your Own Company Secretary, A. J. Scrine, 1987
Business Rip-Offs and How to Avoid Them, Tony Attwood, 1987
Buying for Business: A Guide to Effective Purchasing, Tony Attwood, 1988
Choosing and Using Professional Advisers, 2nd edn, Paul Chaplin, 1986
Debt Collection Made Easy, Peter Buckland, 1988
Export for the Small Business, Henry Deschampsneufs, 1984
Finance and Accounts for Managers, Desmond Goch, 1986
Financial Management for the Small Business: a Daily Telegraph Guide, Colin Barrow, 1984
Going for Growth: A Guide to Corporate Strategy, Michael K. Lawson, 1987
How to Be an Even Better Manager, Michael Armstrong, 1988
How to Buy a Business: The Daily Telegraph Guide, Peter Farrell, 1983
Importing for the Small Business, Mag Morris, 1985
Law for the Small Business: The Daily Telegraph Guide, 5th edition, Patricia Clayton, 1987
Never Take No For an Answer: A Guide to Successful Negotiation, Samfrits Le Poole, 1987
The Practice of Successful Business Management, Kenneth Winckles, 1987
Profits from Improved Productivity, Fiona Halse and John Humphrey, 1988
Raising Finance: the Guardian Guide for the Small Business, 2nd edition, Clive Woodcock, 1985
Successful Expansion for the Small Business: a Daily Telegraph Guide, M. J. Morris, 1984
Taking up a Franchise: The Daily Telegraph Guide, 4th edition, Colin Barrow and Godfrey Golzen
Understand Your Accounts, A. St J. Price, 1986

Index